A PILGRIM'S TESTAMENT

A PILGRIM'S TESTAMENT

THE MEMOIRS OF
IGNATIUS OF LOYOLA

as faithfully transcribed by
LUIS GONÇALVES DA CAMARA
and
newly translated into English by
PARMANANDA R. DIVARKAR

ROME 1983

A PILGRIM'S TESTAMENT

TABLE OF CONTENTS

PRESENTATION

The document whose translation is offered in these pages is generally referred to as the Autobiography of Ignatius of Loyola, for it is a personal account of his life. But it covers only one period — the Pilgrim Years, as they have been called, from the time he left his ancestral home of Loyola after recovering from wounds received in battle, through many wanderings over western Europe and a memorable visit to the Holy Land, till he finally settled down in Rome, to become eventually the first Superior General of the Society of Jesus.

This is an untidy narrative. It seems to be just a patchwork of random memories ranging from the trivial to the profoundly significant, extracted from a reluctant Ignatius by the importunity of devoted friends. He speaks throughout in the third person, about the Pilgrim. That was his self-image: a man on a ceaseless quest, always forging ahead; and not at all inclined to look back, even as he neared journey's end.

But Jerome Nadal, his trusted lieutenant, was determined to obtain a Testament — a piece of fatherly advice, as he explained, such as other Founders of Orders had left to their followers. What he had in mind was not just any kind of pious message, but a practical application of one of his favourite ideas:

namely, that God's ways with Ignatius were the model for God's ways with every Jesuit, and that the Jesuit's response must be patterned on Ignatius' own response. Hence his concern that there be available to the Society of Jesus in all ages an authentic statement of the intimate relationship between God and Ignatius. That would be a Testament indeed; and to produce such a document would be truly to found the Society, said Nadal.

In the language of today, what Nadal and the first Jesuits wanted was an authoritative exposition of the ignatian charism as it must be realized in the Society of Jesus. And in fact the charism does emerge from these Memoirs, and in such a way as to bring to light the coherence of the whole work, and even a certain structured arrangement, in spite of a seemingly haphazard composition, due to the difficult circumstances in which it came into being.

Ignatius had many good reasons for not attempting the task; and when he finally yielded to so many earnest requests, he did not actually write anything. He spoke out his story, in bits and pieces, to Luis Gonçalves da Camara, another loyal companion and a man blessed with a very retentive memory, who first listened with great attention, then ran off to make brief notes, and eventually dictated the text — for the most part in the Spanish used by Ignatius, though this was not the mother-tongue of either of them; and towards the end having to fall back on what passes for Italian in the international community of Rome. In a preface, which is reproduced here, da Camara describes the tremendous odds against which he had to struggle, both as confidant and as transcriber, in order to get the whole job completed. Incidentally, he also betrays a poverty of style on his own part.

It is not surprising that the resulting narrative is most unsatisfactory as a piece of literature. What does come as a surprise is that after it had been obtained at such cost it was never published, either in the original or in translations into modern languages, till the present century. A free Latin version was produced very early, and subsequently printed, but never really circulated. So the facts that are recounted were generally known, but not the text itself — for there seems to have been some embarrassment about the way Ignatius expresses himself, and possibly some disappointment too. Today the document is recognized as a spiritual classic, and as a masterpiece of self-revelation in its very clumsiness.

All of which makes the task of the translator almost impossible. The fundamental problem is what should be the criterion for a good rendering of a bad composition, whose very meaning is sometimes obscure. Da Camara himself says that on occasion he has sacrificed clarity for the sake of faithfulness to the exact words of Ignatius. Presumably the translator should emulate such fidelity even at the risk of damaging his own reputation as a writer. But is it fair to inflict on the reader a painful poverty of vocabulary and grammar, when it is possible to achieve a smoother flow of language without any loss to the sense of what is said?

The principle that has been followed here is to keep to a middle course, leaning towards accuracy rather than elegance, but within the limits of correct and intelligible expression. Idiosyncrasies of style have *generally been preserved. It is hoped that the total impact of the final result retains something of the force and the flavour of the original.*

At the end of the book, some explanatory notes are provided, beginning with an attempt to spell out what was said earlier, that the ignatian charism emerges from the text, and helps to understand the unity and arrangement of the whole composition. Da Camara's own marginal notes, which are regarded as an integral part of the work, though they add very little to it, have all been included. No claim is made that the present effort is more successful than those that have preceded — four so far, in English — but this one has had the advantage of being carried through in Rome, at the Jesuit Headquarters, with all the attendant facilities.

Many colleagues have collaborated in this labour of love, which has served as inspiration during the period of the restoration of the chapel at La Storta, in the outskirts of Rome, which may be said to mark the end of the pilgrimage recorded in these pages. This has also been the time of preparation for the Thirty-Third General Congregation that will give to the Society of Jesus the twenty-eighth successor of Ignatius as Superior General.

So it is to this successor, the Unknown Soldier whose battles are still before him, that we affectionately dedicate our work, with a fond prayer that he and all his companions in the Society of Jesus may share in some measure the experience of Ignatius at La Storta, of being placed with Christ.

PARMANANDA R. DIVARKAR S.J.
Rome, May 20th, 1983

THE PREFACE OF
LUIS GONÇALVES DA CAMARA

The illustration on the reverse, as well as on the cover, shows the signature of Ignatius as it appears on his vote for the election of the first Superior General of the Society of Jesus.

ihno

excluyendo ami mesmo / doy mi noz /
enel Señor nro para feer perlado aaquel
externa mael voz es para feerlo / y he
dado mi determinate bon onfulendo
Sy terme aln ompirma lo pareceran otra
asa /o Jusgare que es Imefor / y amayor
gloria de dios Inro Señor / yo foy
apareJado para Señalar lo el día
en Roma . 5. de abril, de 1541

In the year '53, one Friday morning, the fourth of August, eve of Our Lady of Snows, while the Father was in the garden by the house or apartment known as the Duke's, I began to give him an account of some particulars concerning my soul. Among other things I spoke to him of vainglory. As a remedy the Father told me to refer everything of mine frequently to God, striving to offer him all the good I found in myself, acknowledging it as his and giving him thanks for it. He spoke to me about this in a manner that greatly consoled me, so that I could not restrain my tears. Thus the Father told me how he had been bothered by this vice for two years, so much so that when he embarked from Barcelona for Jerusalem, he did not dare tell anyone that he was going to Jerusalem; and so in other similar instances. And he went on to say how much peace of soul he then felt in this regard.

An hour or two after this we went to dine. While Master Polanco and I were eating with him, the Father said that Master Nadal and others of the Society had often asked something of him, and he had never made up his mind about it. But that after having spoken to me, when he had retired to his room, he had such a devout inclination to do it, and (speaking in a manner that showed that God had greatly enlightened him as to his duty to do so) that he was fully decided on this: to narrate all that had occurred in his soul until now. He had also decided that I should be the one to whom he would reveal these things.

The Father was very ill at that time and never used to promise himself a single day of life. Rather, if someone says, "I will do this a fortnight from now or a week from now," the Father always says with an air of amazement, "What, do you think you will live that long?" And yet this time he said that he expected to live three or four months to finish this business. The next day I spoke to him, asking when he wished us to begin; he replied that I should remind him of it each day (I do not remember how many days) until he was ready for it. But putting it off because of business, he later arranged that I remind him each Sunday. So in September (I do not remember how many days) the Father called me and began to tell me about his whole life and his youthful escapades, clearly and distinctly and with all the details. Later in the same month he called me three or four times and carried his story down to his early days in Manresa, as one may see by the writing in a different hand.

The Father's narrative style is the same that he uses in everything. He speaks with such clarity that he seems to make all that has passed present to one. Therefore, it was not necessary to ask him anything because the Father remembered to tell everything that helped to make one understand. Then, without saying anything to the Father, I went immediately to write it down, first in notes by my own hand and later at greater length, as it is written. I have striven not to put down any words except those that I heard from the

Father. If at all in some things I fear I have failed, it is that in order not to depart from the Father's words, I have not been able to explain adequately the point of some of them.

Thus I wrote this, as said above, until September '53; but from then until Father Nadal came on October 18, '54, the Father was always excusing himself because of some illness or various affairs on hand, saying to me, "When that affair is over, remind me of it;" and when it was over and I reminded him of it, he would say, "We are now with this other; when it is over, remind me of it."

When Father Nadal came, he was very pleased that it was begun but bade me urge the Father, telling me many times that the Father could do nothing of greater benefit for the Society than this, and that this was truly to found the Society. He himself spoke to the Father many times in this way. The Father told me to remind him of it when the business of endowing the College was finished, but after it was done, when the affair of Prester John was finished and the mail had gone.

We got going with the story on the ninth of March, but Pope Julius III began to be in a serious condition at that time and died on the twenty-third, so the Father postponed the matter until there was a pope. There was one, but he also fell ill immediately and died (that was Marcellus). The Father delayed until the election of Pope Paul IV; and afterwards, because of the great heat and his many engagements, postponed it continually until the twenty-first of September when my being sent to Spain began to be discussed. For this reason I strongly pressed the Father to fulfill his promise to me. So now he arranged to do it in the morning of the twenty-second, in the Red Tower. Accordingly, when I had finished saying Mass, I presented myself to him to ask if it was time.

He replied that I should wait for him in the Red Tower, so that when he arrived, I would be there. I took it that I would have to wait for him a long time in that place; and as I tarried at a porch speaking with a brother who had asked me something, the Father came along and reproved me because, failing in obedience, I had not waited for him in the Red Tower. He did not want to do anything that whole day.

Later we were again very insistent with him. So he returned to the Red Tower and dictated pacing about, as he had always done before. In order to observe his face I kept coming a little closer to him, but the Father said to me, "Keep the rule." When, forgetting his remark, I came up to him, failing thus two or three times, the Father repeated the same remark and walked off. At length he returned to the same Tower and finished dictating to me what is written down. But as I was for some time already on the point of undertaking my journey (for the eve of my departure was the last day on which the Father spoke to me about this matter), I could not have everything fully written out in Rome. And not having a Spanish scribe in Genoa, I dictated in Italian whatever I had brought in summary from Rome. I finished the writing in December 1555 at Genoa.

[*In the above Preface by Luis Gonçalves da Camara, the last two paragraphs are missing in the extant copies of the original Spanish text. The manuscripts end abruptly in the middle of the sentence immediately preceding these paragraphs, which are here translated from an early Latin version.*]

THE MEMOIRS OF IGNATIUS OF LOYOLA

Chapter headings have been added to facilitate reading, as well as marginal numbers for ready reference. It is hoped that the Notes at the end of the book will further help to grasp the spirit enshrined in the letter of the text.

Da Camara's marginal notes are indicated by a number, at the proper place in the text, and reproduced at the bottom of the appropriate page.

The illustrations appearing at the beginning of each chapter have been produced by Mariano Ballester on the basis of the wellknown photographs of Leonard von Matt and with the technical assistance of Ján Lukáč.

Chapter 1
PAMPLONA AND LOYOLA
1521-1522

The illustration shows a wall of the castle of
Loyola with the family coat of arms: two wolves at a
cauldron.

1

1   Up to the age of twenty-six he was a man given to the follies of the world; and what he enjoyed most was warlike sport, with a great and foolish desire to win fame.

And so, whilst in a fortress that the French were attacking, when all were of the view that they should surrender, with their lives safeguarded — for they saw clearly that they could not offer resistance — he gave so many reasons to the commander that he actually persuaded him to resist, even against this view of all the officers, who drew courage from his spirit and determination.

When the day came on which the bombardment was expected, he confessed to one of these companions in arms. And after the bombardment had lasted a good while, a shot struck him on one leg, shattering it completely; and as the cannon ball passed between both legs, the other also was badly injured.

2   So with his fall, those in the fortress soon surrendered to the French; who on taking possession

of it, treated the wounded man very well—treated him with courtesy and kindness. And after he had been in Pamplona for twelve or fifteen days, they took him home in a litter.

Here he felt quite unwell. All the doctors and surgeons who were summoned from many places decided that the leg ought to be broken again and the bones reset, saying that because they had been badly set the other time, or it had got broken on the road, they were out of place, and this way he could not mend. And once again this butchery was gone through; during it, as in all the others he underwent before or after, he never said a word nor showed any sign of pain other than to clench his fists tightly.

3   Yet he kept getting worse, not being able to eat, and with the other symptoms that usually point to death. When St John's day came, because the doctors were far from confident about his health, he was advised to confess; he received the sacraments on the eve of St Peter and St Paul. The doctors said that if he did not feel any improvement by midnight, he could be taken for dead. It happened that this sick man was devoted to St Peter; so Our Lord deigned that he should begin to get better that very midnight. His improvement proceeded so well that some days later it was judged that he was out of danger of death.

4   And his bones having knit together, one bone below the knee was left riding on another, which made the leg shorter. The bone protruded so

much that it was an ugly business. He could not bear such a thing because he was set on a worldly career and thought that this would deform him; he asked the surgeons if it could be cut away. They said that it could indeed be cut away, but that the pain would be greater than all that he had suffered, because it was already healed and it would take a while to cut it. And yet he chose on his own to make himself a martyr, though his elder brother was shocked and said that he himself would not dare suffer such pain; but the wounded man bore it with his wonted endurance.

5 After the flesh and excess bone were cut away, remedial measures were taken that the leg might not be so short; ointment was often applied, and it was stretched continually with instruments that tortured him for many days. But Our Lord kept giving him health; and he felt so well that he was quite fit except that he could not stand easily on his leg and had perforce to stay in bed.

As he was much given to reading worldly books of fiction, commonly labelled chivalry, when he felt better he asked to be given some of them to pass the time. But in that house none of those that he usually read could be found, so they gave him a Life of Christ and a book of the lives of the saints in Castilian.

6 As he read them over many times, he became rather fond of what he found written there. But interrupting his reading, he sometimes stopped to think about the things he had read and at other

times about the things of the world that he used to think of before. Of the many foolish ideas that occurred to him, one had taken such a hold on his heart that he was absorbed in thinking about it for two and three and four hours without realizing it: he imagined what he would do in the service of a certain lady; the means he would take so he could go to the place where she lived; the quips — the words he would address to her; the feats of arms he would perform in her service. He became so infatuated with this that he did not consider how impossible of attainment it would be, because the lady was not of ordinary nobility; not a countess nor a duchess; but her station was higher than any of these.

7   Nevertheless Our Lord assisted him, causing other thoughts, that arose from the things he read, to follow these. For in reading the life of Our Lord and of the saints, he stopped to think, reasoning within himself, "What if I should do this which St Francis did; and this which St Dominic did?" Thus he pondered over many things that he found good, always proposing to himself what was difficult and burdensome; and as he so proposed, it seemed easy for him to accomplish it. But he did no more than argue within himself, saying, "St Dominic did this, therefore I have to do it; St Francis did this, therefore I have to do it."

These thoughts also lasted a good while; then, other things coming in between, the worldly ones mentioned above returned, and he also stayed long with them. This succession of such diverse thoughts lasted for quite some time, and he always dwelt at length on the thought that turned up, either of the worldly exploits he wished to perform or of these others of God that came to his imagination, until he tired of it and put it aside and turned to other matters.

8   Yet there was this difference. When he was think-ing of those things of the world, he took much delight in them, but afterwards, when he was tired and put them aside, he found himself dry and dissatisfied. But when he thought of going to Jerusalem barefoot, and of eating nothing but plain vegetables and of practising all the other rigours that he saw in the saints, not only was he consoled when he had these thoughts, but even after putting them aside he remained satisfied and joyful.

He did not notice this, however; nor did he stop to ponder the distinction until the time when his eyes were opened a little, and he began to marvel at the difference and to reflect upon it, realizing from experience that some thoughts left him sad and others joyful. Little by little he came to recognize the difference between the spirits that were stirring, one from the devil, the other from God.[1]

_____

[1] This was his first reflection on the things of God; and later, when he composed the Exercises, this was his starting point in clari-fying the matter of diversity of spirits.

9   From this lesson he derived not a little light, and he began to think more earnestly about his past life and about the great need he had to do penance for it. At this point the desire to imitate the saints came to him, though he gave no thought to details, only promising with God's grace to do as they had done. But the one thing he wanted to do was to go to Jerusalem as soon as he recovered, as mentioned above, with as much of disciplines and fasts as a generous spirit, fired with God, would want to perform.

10   And so he began to forget the previous thoughts, with these holy desires he had, and they were confirmed by a spiritual experience, in this manner. One night while he was awake, he saw clearly an image of Our Lady with the holy Child Jesus. From this sight he received for a considerable time very great consolation, and he was left with such loathing for his whole past life and especially for the things of the flesh, that it seemed to him that his spirit was rid of all the images that had been painted on it. Thus from that hour until August '53 when this was written, he never gave the slightest consent to the things of the flesh. For this reason it may be considered the work of God, although he did not dare to claim it nor said more than to affirm the above. But his brother as well as all the rest of the household came to know from his exterior the change that had been wrought inwardly in his soul.

11 With not a care, he persevered in his reading and his good resolutions; and all his time of conversation with members of the household he spent on the things of God; thus he benefited their souls. As he very much liked those books, the idea came to him to note down briefly some of the more essential things from the life of Christ and the saints; so he set himself very diligently to write a book (because he was now beginning to be up and about the house a bit) with red ink for the words of Christ, blue ink for those of Our Lady, on polished and lined paper, in a good hand because he was a very fine penman[2].

Part of the time he spent in writing and part in prayer. The greatest consolation he experienced was gazing at the sky and the stars, which he often did and for long, because he thus felt within himself a very great impulse to serve Our Lord. He often thought about his intention and wished he were now wholly well so he could get on his way.

12 And taking stock of what he might do after he returned from Jerusalem, so he could always live as a penitent, he thought he might enter the Carthusian house in Seville, without saying who he was, so that they would make little of him; and there never to eat anything but plain vegetables. But when he thought again of the penances he

---

[2] This had nearly 300 pages, all written, quarto size.

wished to do as he went about the world, the desire to enter the Carthusians cooled, with the fear that he would not be able to give vent to the hatred that he had conceived against himself. Still he instructed one of the household servants who was going to Burgos to get information about the rule of the Carthusians, and the information he obtained about it seemed good.

But for the reason mentioned above and because he was wholly absorbed in the journey he was planning soon to make, and that matter did not have to be dealt with until his return, he did not look much into it. Rather, finding now that he had some strength, he thought the time to depart had come; and he said to his brother, "Sir, the Duke of Nájera, as you know, is aware now that I am well. It will be good that I go to Navarrete." (The duke was there at that time.)[3]

His brother took him to one room and then another, and with much feeling begged him not to throw himself away and to consider what hopes had been placed in him by the people, and how much he could achieve, and other such words, all with the purpose of dissuading him from his good intention. But he answered in such a way that, without departing from the truth, for he was now very scrupulous about that, he slipped away from his brother.

---

[3] His brother and others at home suspected he was planning some drastic change.

Chapter 2
ROAD TO MONTSERRAT
1522

The illustration is of the popular Black Virgin of Montserrat, before whom Ignatius kept his vigil of arms.

2

13 And so, as he mounted a mule, another brother wished to go with him as far as Oñate. On the road he persuaded him to join in a vigil at Our Lady of Aránzazu. That night he prayed there that he might gain fresh strength for his journey. He left his brother in Oñate at the house of a sister he was going to visit, and himself went on to Navarrete[4].

Remembering that a few ducats were owed him at the duke's household, he thought it would be well to collect them; for this he wrote out a bill for the treasurer. The treasurer said he had no money; and the duke hearing this said there might be a lack for everything but no lacking for Loyola — to whom he wanted to give a good position, if he would accept it, because of the reputation he had earned in the past. He collected the money and arranged that it be distributed among certain

---

[4] From the day he left home, he always took the discipline each night.

persons to whom he felt indebted, with a part for a statue of Our Lady that was in ill repair, so it could be repaired and handsomely adorned. Then dismissing the two servants who had come with him, he set out alone on his mule from Navarrete for Montserrat.

14 On the way something happened to him which it would be well to record, so one may understand how Our Lord dealt with this soul, which was still blind, though greatly desirous of serving him as far as his knowledge went. Thus, he decided to do great penances, no longer with an eye to satisfying for his sins so much as to please and gratify God. So when it occurred to him to do some penance that the saints practised, he determined to do the same and even more[5].

From these thoughts he derived all his consolation, not looking to any interior thing, nor knowing what humility was, or charity or patience; or the discretion that regulates and measures these virtues. His whole intention was to do such great external works because the saints had done so for the glory of God, without considering any more particular detail.

15 Well, as he was going on his way, a Moor came

---

[5] He had such disgust of his past sins, and such a lively desire to do great things for love of God, that though he made no judgement that his sins were forgiven, he did not give them much attention in the penances that he undertook to perform.

up to him riding on a mule. They went along chatting together and got to talking about Our Lady; and the Moor said it seemed to him that the Virgin had indeed conceived without a man, but he could not believe in her giving birth remaining a virgin. In support of this he cited the natural arguments that suggested themselves to him. The pilgrim, in spite of the many reasons he gave him, could not dislodge this opinion. The Moor then went ahead so quickly that he lost sight of him, and he was left pondering over what had transpired with the Moor.

At this, various emotions came over him and caused discontent in his soul, as it seemed that he had not done his duty. They also aroused his indignation against the Moor, for it seemed that he had done wrong in allowing the Moor to say such things about Our Lady, and that he ought to sally forth in defense of her honour. He felt inclined to go in search of the Moor and stab him with his dagger for what he had said. After a long engagement in this struggle of inclinations, he remained uncertain at the end, not knowing what he ought to do. The Moor, who had moved ahead, had told him that he was going to a place a little farther on the same road, very near the highway, though the highway did not pass through the place.

16 So, being tired of examining what would be best to do and not arriving at a definite conclusion, he decided as follows: to let the mule go with the reins slack as far as the place where the ways

parted. And if the mule took the village road, he would seek out the Moor and stab him; if the mule did not go toward the village but took the highway, he would let him be. And doing as he had thought, Our Lord deigned that although the village was little more than thirty or forty paces away, and the road to it was very broad and very good, the mule took the highway and left the village road.

Coming to a large town before Montserrat, he decided to buy there the attire he had resolved to wear—and use when going to Jerusalem. He bought cloth from which sacks are usually made, loosely woven and very prickly. Then he ordered a long garment to be made from it, reaching to his feet. He bought a pilgrim's staff and a small gourd and put everything in front by the mule's saddle[6].

17   He went on his way to Montserrat, thinking as he always did of the exploits he would perform for the love of God. And as his mind was all full of tales like Amadis de Gaul and such books, the ideas that came to him were along those lines. Thus he decided to keep a vigil of arms one whole night, without sitting or lying down, but standing

---

[6] He also bought some slippers, of which he took just one; and this not for style but because he had one leg all tied up with a bandage and somewhat neglected, so much so that though he was mounted, each night he found it swollen; this foot he thought must be shod.

a while and kneeling a while, before the altar of Our Lady of Montserrat, where he had resolved to lay aside his garments and to don the armour of Christ. So leaving this place, he set off, thinking as usual of his resolutions.

On arrival at Montserrat, after praying and fixing an appointment with the confessor, he made a general confession in writing; it lasted three days. He arranged with the confessor to have his mule taken in charge, and his sword and dagger placed in the church at the altar of Our Lady. This was the first man to whom he revealed his decision, because until then he had not revealed it to any confessor.

18 On the eve of Our Lady in March, at night, in the year 1522, he went as secretly as he could to a beggar—and stripping off all his garments he gave them to a beggar; he dressed himself in his chosen attire and went to kneel before the altar of Our Lady. At times in this way, at other times standing, with his pilgrim's staff in his hand, he spent the whole night.

He left at daybreak so as not to be recognized, and did not take the road that led straight to Barcelona, where he would come across many who would recognize and honour him, but turned off to a town called Manresa. Here he planned to stay in a hospice a few days—and also to note some things in his book; this he carried around very carefully, and he was greatly consoled by it.

As he was gone about a league from Montserrat, a man who had been hurrying after him, caught up and asked if he had given some clothes to a beggar, as the beggar affirmed. Answering that he had, tears flowed from his eyes in compassion for the beggar to whom he had given the clothes — in compassion, for he realized they were harassing him, thinking he had stolen them.

Yet as much as he avoided favourable notice, he could not remain long in Manresa before people had a big story to tell — their ideas coming from what happened at Montserrat; and soon the tale grew into saying more than the truth: that he had given up a large income, etc.

CHAPTER 3
SOJOURN AT MANRESA
1522-1523

The illustration presents a view of Manresa: the little church of Santa Maria de Viladordis, often visited by Ignatius.

3

19 He begged alms in Manresa every day. He did not eat meat nor drink wine, even though they were offered to him. He did not fast on Sundays, and if they gave him a little wine, he drank it. Because he had been very fastidious in taking care of his hair, as was the fashion at that time (and his was handsome), he decided to let it go its way according to nature without combing or cutting it or covering it with anything by night or day. For the same reason he let the nails grow on toes and fingers because he had been fastidious in this too.

While in this hospice it often happened that in broad daylight he saw something in the air near him. It gave him great consolation because it was very beautiful — remarkably so. He could not discern very well the kind of thing it was, but in a way it seemed to him to have the form of a serpent with many things that shone like eyes, though they were not. He found great pleasure and consolation in seeing this thing, and the oftener he saw it the more his consolation grew. When it disappeared, he was displeased.

20   Until this time he had remained always in nearly the same interior state of very steady joy, without having any knowledge of interior things of the spirit. The days while that vision lasted or somewhat before it began (for it lasted many days), a forceful thought came to trouble him by pointing out the hardships of his life, like a voice within his soul, "How will you be able to endure this life for the seventy years you have to live?" Sensing that it was from the enemy, he answered interiorly with great vehemence, "Wretch! Can you promise me an hour of life?" So he overcame the temptation and remained at peace. This was the first temptation that came to him after what is mentioned above. It happened when he was entering a church where he heard High Mass each day and Vespers and Compline, all sung, finding in this great comfort. Usually he read the Passion at Mass, always retaining his serenity.

21   But soon after the temptation noted above, he began to have great changes in his soul. Sometimes he felt so out of sorts that he found no relish in saying prayers nor in hearing Mass nor in any other devotion he might practise. At other times quite the opposite of this came over him so suddenly that he seemed to have thrown off sadness and desolation just as one snatches a cape from another's shoulders. Now he started getting perturbed by these changes that he had never experienced before, and he said to himself, "What new life is this that we are now beginning"?

At this time he still conversed occasionally

with spiritual persons who had regard for him and wanted to talk to him, because even though he had no knowledge of spiritual matters, yet in his speech he revealed great fervour and eagerness to go forward in God's service. At that time there was at Manresa a woman of great age, with a long record also as a servant of God, and known as such in many parts of Spain, so much so that the Catholic King had summoned her once to communicate something. One day this woman, speaking to the new soldier of Christ, said to him, "O! May my Lord Jesus Christ deign to appear to you some day." But he was startled at this, taking the matter quite literally, "How would Jesus Christ appear to me?" He persevered steadily in his usual confession and communion each Sunday.

22 But here he began to have much trouble from scruples, for even though the general confession he had made at Montserrat had been quite carefully done and all in writing, as has been said, still at times it seemed to him that he had not confessed certain things. This caused him much distress, because although he confessed that, he was not satisfied. Thus he began to look for some spiritual men who could cure him of these scruples, but nothing helped him. Finally, a doctor of the cathedral, a very spiritual man who preached there, told him one day in confession to write down everything he could remember. He did so, but after confession the scruples still returned, becoming increasingly minute so that he was in great distress.

Although he was practically convinced that those scruples did him much harm and that it would be good to be rid of them, he could not break himself off. Sometimes he thought it would cure him if his confessor ordered him in the name of Jesus Christ not to confess anything of the past; he wanted his confessor to order him thus, but he did not dare say this to his confessor.

23 But without his saying so, his confessor ordered him not to confess anything of the past, unless it was something quite clear. But since he found all those things to be very clear, this order was of no use to him, and so he continued with the difficulty. At this time he was staying in a small room that the Dominicans had given him in their monastery. He persevered in his seven hours of prayer on his knees, getting up regularly at midnight, and in all the other exercises mentioned earlier. But in none of them did he find any cure for his scruples; and it was many months that they were tormenting him.

Once when he was very distressed by them, he began to pray, and roused to fervour he shouted out loud to God, saying, "Help me, Lord, for I find no remedy in men nor in any creature; yet if I thought I could find it, no labour would be hard for me. Yourself, Lord, show me where I may find it; even though I should have to chase after a puppy that it may give me the remedy, I will do it."

24   While he had these thoughts, the temptation often
      came over him with great force to throw himself
      through a large hole in his room, next to the
      place where he was praying. But realizing that it
      was a sin to kill oneself, he shouted again, "Lord,
      I will do nothing that offends you," repeating
      these words many times, as well as the previous
      ones. Then there came to his mind the story of a
      saint who, in order to obtain from God something
      that he wanted very much, went without eating
      many days until he got it. Thinking about this for
      a good while, he at last decided to do it, telling
      himself that he would not eat nor drink until God
      succoured him, or until he saw that death was
      quite close — for should it happen that he found
      himself at the extreme limit, so that he would
      soon die if he did not eat, then he thought to ask
      for bread and to eat (as if indeed at that limit he
      would be able to ask or to eat).

25   This happened one Sunday after he had received
      communion; he persevered the whole week
      without putting anything into his mouth, not
      ceasing to do his usual exercises, even going to
      divine office and saying his prayers on his knees,
      even at midnight, etc. But when the next Sunday
      came and he had to go to confession, since he
      used to tell his confessor in great detail what he
      had done, he also told him how he had eaten
      nothing during that week. His confessor ordered
      him to break that fast; and though he still felt
      strong, he nevertheless obeyed his confessor, and
      that day and the next he felt free from scruples.

But on the third day, which was Tuesday, while at prayer he began to remember his sins; and so, as in a process of threading, he went on thinking of sin after sin from his past and felt he was obliged to confess them again. But after these thoughts, disgust for the life he led came over him, with impulses to give it up.

In this way the Lord deigned that he awake as from sleep. As he now had some experience of the diversity of spirits from the lessons God had given him, he began to examine the means by which that spirit had come. He thus decided with great lucidity not to confess anything from the past anymore; and so from that day forward he remained free of those scruples and held it for certain that Our Lord had mercifully deigned to deliver him.

26   Besides his seven hours of prayer he busied himself helping in spiritual matters certain souls who came there looking for him. All the rest of the day he spent thinking about the things of God that he had meditated upon or read that day. But when he went to bed, great enlightenment, great spiritual consolations, often came to him; so that they made him lose much of the time he had allotted to sleep, which was not much. Examining this several times, he thought to himself that he had ample time assigned for converse with God, and all the rest of the day as well; and he began to doubt, therefore, whether that enlightenment came from a good spirit. He concluded that it

would be better to ignore it and to sleep for the allotted time. And so he did.

27 He continued to abstain from eating meat and was so determined about it that he would not think of changing it for any reason; but one day, when he got up in the morning, edible meat appeared before him as if he saw it with his ordinary eyes, though no desire for it had preceded. At the same time he also had a strong inclination of his will to eat it from then on. Although he remembered his previous intention, he had no doubt about this, but rather a conviction that he ought to eat meat. Later when telling this to his confessor, the confessor told him to consider whether perhaps this was a temptation; but examining it carefully, never could he doubt about it.

God treated him at this time just as a schoolmaster treats a child whom he is teaching. Whether this was because of his lack of education and of brains, or because he had no one to teach him, or because of the strong desire God himself had given him to serve him, he believed without doubt and has always believed that God treated him in this way. Indeed if he were to doubt this, he would think he offended his Divine Majesty. Something of this can be seen from the five following points.

28 FIRST. He had great devotion to the Most Holy Trinity, and so each day he prayed to the three Persons separately. But as he also prayed to the Most Holy Trinity, the thought came to him: why

did he say four prayers to the Trinity? But this thought gave him little or no difficulty, being hardly important. One day while saying the Office of Our Lady on the steps of the same monastery, his understanding began to be elevated so that he saw the Most Holy Trinity in the form of three musical keys. This brought on so many tears and so much sobbing that he could not control himself. That morning, while going in a procession that set out from there, he could not hold back his tears until dinnertime; nor after eating could he stop talking about the Most Holy Trinity, using many comparisons in great variety and with much joy and consolation. As a result, the effect has remained with him throughout his life of experiencing great devotion while praying to the Most Holy Trinity.

29   SECOND. Once, the manner in which God had created the world was presented to his understanding with great spiritual joy. He seemed to see something white, from which some rays were coming, and God made light from this. But he did not know how to explain these things, nor did he remember too well the spiritual enlightenment that God was imprinting on his soul at the time.

THIRD. At Manresa too, where he stayed almost a year, after he began to be consoled by God, and saw the fruit which he bore in dealing with souls, he gave up those extremes he had formerly practised, and he now cut his nails and his hair. One day in this town while he was hearing Mass in the church of the monastery mentioned above, at the elevation of the Body of the Lord, he saw with interior eyes something like white rays coming from above. Although he cannot explain this very well after so long a time, nevertheless what he saw clearly with his understanding was how Jesus Christ our Lord was there in that Most Holy Sacrament.

FOURTH. Often and for a long time, while at prayer, he saw with interior eyes the humanity of Christ. The form that appeared to him was like a white body, neither very large nor very small, but he did not see any distinction of members. He saw it at Manresa many times. If he should say twenty or forty, he would not dare judge it a lie. He has seen this another time in Jerusalem and yet another while travelling near Padua. He has also seen Our Lady in a similar form, without distinguishing parts. These things he saw strengthened him then and always gave him such strength in his faith that he has often thought to himself: if there were no Scriptures to teach us these matters of faith, he would be resolved to die for them, solely because of what he has seen.

30 FIFTH. Once he was going out of devotion to a church situated a little more than a mile from Manresa; I believe it is called St Paul's, and the road goes by the river. As he went along occupied with his devotions, he sat down for a little while with his face toward the river, which ran down below. While he was seated there, the eyes of his understanding began to be opened; not that he saw any vision, but he understood and learnt

many things, both spiritual matters and matters of faith and of scholarship, and this with so great an enlightenment that everything seemed new to him.[7]

The details that he understood then, though there were many, cannot be stated, but only that he experienced a great clarity in his understanding. This was such that in the whole course of his life, after completing sixty-two years, even if he gathered up all the various helps he may have had from God and all the various things he has known, even adding them all together, he does not think he had got as much as at that one time.

31 After this had lasted for a good while, he went to kneel before a nearby cross to give thanks to God. There, the vision that had appeared to him many times but which he had never understood, that is, the thing mentioned above which seemed very beautiful to him, with many eyes, now appeared to him. But while before the cross, he saw clearly that the object did not have its usual beautiful colour, and he knew very clearly with a strong agreement of his will that it was the devil. Later it would often appear to him for a long time; and by way of contempt he dispelled it with a staff he used to carry in his hand.

32 Once while he was ill at Manresa, a very severe

---

[7] This left his understanding so very enlightened that he felt as if he were another man with another mind.

fever brought him to the point of death, and he fully believed that his soul was about to leave him. At this a thought came to him telling him that he was a just man, but this caused him so much trouble that he constantly rejected it and called his sins to mind. He had more trouble with this thought than with the fever itself, but no matter how much trouble he took to overcome the thought, he could not overcome it. Then somewhat relieved of the fever, he was no longer at the point of expiring, and he began to shout loudly to some ladies who had come there to visit him, that for the love of God, when they next saw him at the point of death, they should shout at him with loud voices, addressing him as sinner: let him remember the offences he had committed against God.

33 Another time, while going by sea from Valencia to Italy in a violent storm, the rudder of the ship was broken, and the situation reached such a pass that in his judgement and that of many others who sailed on the ship, they could not by natural means escape death. At this time, examining himself carefully and preparing to die, he could not feel afraid for his sins or of being condemned, but he did feel embarrassment and sorrow, as he believed he had not used well the gifts and graces which God our Lord had granted him.

Another time, in the year '50, he was very bad with a very severe illness which, in his opinion as well as of many others, would be the last. At this time, thinking about death, he felt such joy and such spiritual consolation at having to die that he dissolved entirely into tears. This became so habitual that he often stopped thinking about death so as not to feel so much of that consolation.

34   When winter came he was down with a very severe illness, and for treatment the town put him in a house of the father of one Ferrera, who was later in the service of Baltasar de Faria. There he was cared for with great attention; and many prominent ladies, because of the deep regard they now had for him, came to watch over him by night. Though he recovered from this illness, he was still very weak and with frequent stomach pains. For these reasons, therefore, and because the winter was very cold, they made him dress up and wear shoes and cover his head; so they made him use two brown jackets of very coarse cloth and a cap of the same, something like a beret. At this time there was a long period during which he was very eager to converse on spiritual matters and to find persons who could deal with them. Meanwhile, the time was approaching when he planned to set out for Jerusalem.

35   So at the beginning of the year ˮ23 he set out for Barcelona to take ship. Although various people offered to accompany him, he wanted to go quite alone, for his whole idea was to have God alone as refuge. One day when some were urging strongly, because he did not know either the Italian or the Latin languages, that he have a companion, telling him how much this would help

him and praising the person highly, he said that he would not go even in the company of the son or the brother of the Duke of Cardona, because he wanted to practise three virtues—charity, faith, and hope. If he took a companion, he would expect help from him when he was hungry; if he fell down, the man would help him get up; and so also he would trust him and feel attachment to him on this account; but he wanted to place that trust, attachment, and expectation in God alone.

What he said in this way, he felt just so in his heart. With these thoughts, he not only had the desire to set out alone but to go without any provisions. When he began to arrange for his passage, he got round the master of the ship to carry him free, as he had no money, but on condition that he brought to the ship some biscuit for his sustenance; otherwise, for nothing in the world would they accept him.

36   When he went to obtain the biscuit, great scruples came over him: "Is this the hope and faith you had in God who would not fail you?" etc. This was so powerful as to trouble him greatly; at last, not knowing what to do because he saw probable reasons on both sides, he decided to place himself in the hands of his confessor. So he told him how much he wanted to seek perfection and whatever would be more to the glory of God, and the reasons that caused him to doubt whether he ought to take any provisions. The confessor decided that he should beg what was necessary and take it with him.

As he begged from a lady, she asked where he was planning to travel. He hesitated a bit whether he would tell her, but at last he ventured to say no more than that he was going to Italy and to Rome. And as if in amazement, she said, "You want to go to Rome? Well, I don't know how those who go there come back." (She meant to say that in Rome one profited little in spiritual things.) Now the reason why he did not dare say that he was going to Jerusalem was fear of vainglory. This fear haunted him so, he never dared say to what country or to what family he belonged. At last, having the biscuit, he went on board. But at the shore he found he had five or six *blancas* left from what he was given begging from door to door (for he used to live that way); he left them on a bench that he came across there by the shore.

37 So he embarked, having been in Barcelona a little more than twenty days. While he was still in Barcelona before embarking, he sought out, as was his practice, all spiritual persons, even though they lived in hermitages far from the city, to converse with them. But neither in Barcelona nor in Manresa during the whole time he was there did he find persons who could help him as much as he wished; only in Manresa that woman mentioned above, who told him she prayed God that Jesus Christ might appear to him: she alone seemed to him to enter more deeply into spiritual matters. Therefore, after leaving Barcelona, he completely lost this eagerness to seek out spiritual persons.

CHAPTER 4
PILGRIMAGE TO JERUSALEM
1523

The illustration shows a stretch of the Way of the Cross in Jerusalem, at the Fifth Station: Simon of Cyrene helps Jesus.

4

38 They had such a strong wind at the stern that they reached Gaeta from Barcelona in five days and nights, though they were all thoroughly frightened because of very rough weather. Throughout all that region there was fear of the plague; but as soon as he disembarked he began the journey to Rome. Of those who came on the ship, a mother and her daughter whom she had in boy's clothing, and another youth, accompanied him. They joined him because they also were begging.

Having reached a lodge, they came upon a great blaze with many soldiers at it, who gave them to eat, and a good deal of wine, coaxing them as if they wanted to warm them up. Later they separated them, the mother and daughter being placed in a room above and the pilgrim and the youth in a stable. But at midnight, he heard loud cries from that quarter, above; getting up to see what it was, he found the mother and her daughter in the courtyard below, wailing and complaining that there was an attempt to violate them. At this such a strong feeling came over him that he began to shout, saying: "Must one put up with this?" and similar protests. He uttered these words with such force that all those in the house were alarmed. No one did him any harm. The youth had already fled, and though it was still night, all three got going.

39 When they arrived at a nearby city, they found it closed. Unable to enter, the three of them spent the night in a leaky church there. In the morning they would not allow them into the city, and they found no alms outside, even though they went to a castle which could be seen nearby. There the pilgrim felt weak because of the hardships on the sea as well as all else, etc.; unable to travel farther, he remained there. The mother and her daughter went on to Rome.

That day many people came out of the city; learning that the Lady of the place was coming there, he approached her saying that he was ill only from weakness and asked her to let him enter the city to seek some cure. She readily granted it, and he began to beg through the city and obtained a fair amount. After two days of recovery there, he set out on his journey again and arrived in Rome on Palm Sunday.

40 Here all who spoke to him, on discovering that he did not carry any money for Jerusalem, began to dissuade him from making that trip, asserting with many arguments that it was impossible to find passage without money. But he had great

assurance in his soul and he could not doubt but that he would in fact find a way to go to Jerusalem. After receiving the blessing of Pope Adrian VI, he set out for Venice eight or nine days after Easter. He did have six or seven ducats which had been given him for the passage from Venice to Jerusalem; he had accepted them, being somewhat overcome by the fears suggested to him that he would not otherwise make the passage. But two days after leaving Rome, he began to realize that this was a lack of trust on his part, and it greatly bothered him that he had accepted the ducats, so he wondered if it would be good to be rid of them. He finally decided to give them generously to those who approached him, who were beggars usually. He so managed that when he eventually arrived in Venice, he had no more than a small amount which he required that night.

41 While on the journey to Venice, he slept in doorways because of the guards against the plague. It happened once that when he got up in the morning he ran into a man who, with one look, fled in horror, presumably because he saw him so very pale. Travelling in this way, he came to Chioggia, and with some companions who had joined him, he learned that they would not be allowed to enter Venice. His companions decided to go to Padua to obtain a certificate of health there, so he set out with them. But he could not keep up for they went very fast, leaving him at nightfall in a large field.

   While he was there, Christ appeared to him in

the manner in which he usually appeared to him, as we have mentioned above, and this brought him much comfort. Consoled in this way, the next morning, without forging a certificate as (I believe) his companions had done, he came to the gates of Padua and entered without the guards asking anything of him. The same thing happened when he left. This greatly astonished his companions who had just got a certificate to go to Venice, about which he did not bother

42 When they arrived at Venice, the guards came to the boat to examine them all, one by one, as many as were in it, but him alone they let be. He maintained himself in Venice by begging, and he slept in St Mark's Square. But he would never go to the house of the Emperor's ambassador, nor did he take any special care to seek the means for his passage. He had a great assurance in his soul that God would provide a way for him to go to Jerusalem; this gave him such confidence that no arguments or fears suggested to him could make him doubt.

One day he ran into a rich Spaniard who asked him what he was doing and where he wanted to go. Learning his purpose, the man took him home to dinner, and kept him a few days till all was set for the departure. Ever since Manresa the pilgrim had the habit when he ate with anyone, never to speak at table except to answer briefly; but he listened to what was said and noted some things which he took as the occasion to speak about God, and when the meal was finished, he did so.

43   This was the reason why the worthy gentleman
and all his household were so attached to him and
wanted him to stay and made an effort to keep
him there. This same host brought him to the
Doge of Venice so he could speak to him; that is,
he obtained entrance and an audience for him.
When the Doge heard the pilgrim, he ordered that
he be given passage on the ship of the governors
who were going to Cyprus.

Although many pilgrims had come that year
for Jerusalem, most of them had returned home
because of the recent event which had occurred,
the capture of Rhodes. Even so there were thirteen on the pilgrim ship which sailed first, and
eight or nine remained for the governors' ship.

As this was about to leave, our pilgrim had a
severe bout of fever; but after troubling him a few
days, it left him. The ship was sailing on the day
he had taken a purge. The people of the house
asked the doctor if he could embark for
Jerusalem, and the doctor said that indeed he
could embark, if he wanted to be buried there.
But he did embark and sail that day; and he
vomited in such a way that he felt much relieved
and began to recover completely.

He severely condemned some obscenities and
indecencies that were openly practised on the ship.

44   The Spaniards who were there warned him not to
do so, because the ship's crew were planning to
leave him on some island. But Our Lord deigned
that they arrive quickly at Cyprus. Leaving the
ship there, they went overland to another port
called Las Salinas, ten leagues away. They board-

ed the pilgrim ship, on which also he brought no more for his maintenance than his hope in God, as he had done on the other.

During all this time, Our Lord appeared to him often, giving him great consolation and determination; but what he seemed to see was something round and large, as though it were of gold: and this was what presented itself to him.

Having left Cyprus they arrived at Jaffa. Moving on to Jerusalem on their little donkeys, as is usually done, two miles before they reached Jerusalem a Spaniard — a noble it would seem, named Diego Manes — suggested with great devotion to all the pilgrims that since in a little while they would reach the place from which they could see the Holy City, it would be well for all to prepare their consciences and go in silence.

45   This seemed good to them all, and each one began to recollect himself. A little before coming to the place from where it could be seen, they dismounted, because they saw the friars with the cross, awaiting them. On seeing the city the pilgrim felt great consolation; and as the others testified, this was common to them all, with a joy that did not seem natural. He always felt this same devotion on his visits to the holy places.

His firm intention was to remain in Jerusalem, continually visiting those holy places; and in addition to this devotion, he also planned to help souls. For this purpose he had brought letters of recommendation for the Guardian and gave them to him. He told him of his intention to remain there because of his devotion; but not the second part, about wanting to help souls, because he had not told this to anyone, whilst he had frequently made public the first. The Guardian answered that he did not see how he could stay because the house was in such need that it could not support the friars; for that reason he had decided to send some with the pilgrims, to these parts. The pilgrim replied that he wanted nothing from the house, except only that when he came sometimes to confess, they would hear his confession. With that the Guardian told him that such an arrangement might work, but he would have to wait for the coming of the Provincial (I believe he was the head of the order in that area), who was at Bethlehem.

46 By this promise the pilgrim was reassured and began to write letters to Barcelona to spiritual persons. Having already written one and while writing another on the eve of the departure of the pilgrims, he received a summons from the Provincial (for he had arrived) and the Guardian. The Provincial spoke kindly to him, saying that he knew of his good intention to remain in those holy places, and he had given much thought to the matter; but because of the experience he had had with others, he judged that it was not expedient. For many had had that desire, but some had been captured and others killed, and the order had later been obliged to ransom the captives. Therefore he should prepare to leave the next day with the pilgrims.

He replied to this that he was very firm in his purpose and was resolved that on no account would he fail to carry it out. He frankly gave them to understand that even though the Provincial thought otherwise, if there was nothing binding him under sin, he would not abandon his intention out of any fear. To this the Provincial replied that they had authority from the Apostolic See to have anyone leave the place, or remain there, as they judged, and to excommunicate anyone who was unwilling to obey them; and that in this case they thought that he should not remain, etc.

47 He wanted to show him the bulls giving them power to excommunicate, but he said he did not need to see them, as he believed their reverences; inasmuch as they had so decided with the authority they had, he would obey them. When this was over, returning to where he had been before, he felt a strong desire to visit Mount Olivet again before leaving, since it was not Our Lord's will that he remain in those holy places. On Mount Olivet there is a stone from which Our Lord rose up to heaven, and his footprints are still seen there; this was what he wanted to see again.

So without saying anything or taking a guide (for those who go without a Turk as guide run a great risk), he slipped away from the others and went alone to Mount Olivet. But the guards would not let him enter. He gave them a penknife that he carried, and after praying with great consolation, he felt the desire to go to Bethphage.

While there he remembered that he had not noted on Mount Olivet on what side the right foot was, or on what side the left. Returning there, I think he gave his scissors to the guards so they would let him enter.

48 When it was learned in the monastery that he had gone like that without a guide, the friars took steps to find him. So as he was coming down from Mount Olivet he ran into a "belted" Christian who served in the monastery. He had a large staff and with a great show of annoyance made as if to strike him. When he came up to him he grabbed him tightly by the arm, and he readily let himself be led. The good man, however, never let him go. As he went along this way, held thus by the "belted" Christian, he felt great consolation from Our Lord, and it seemed to him that he saw Christ over him continually. This lasted all through in great abundance until he reached the monastery.

The illustration is of an old quarter of Barcelona: the house of Isabel Roser by the side of the church where she first met Ignatius.

5

49 The next day they set out, and after arriving at Cyprus, the pilgrims dispersed in different ships. In the port there were three or four ships bound for Venice. One was Turkish, another was a very small vessel, and the third was a very rich and powerful ship belonging to a wealthy Venetian. Some pilgrims asked the master of this ship kindly to take the pilgrim; but when he learned that he had no money, he did not want to, even though many made petition, praising him, etc. The master answered that if he was a saint, he should travel as St James had done, or something like that. These same petitioners very easily succeeded with the master of the small vessel.

They set out one day with a good wind in the morning; but in the afternoon a storm came upon them, and they got separated one from the other. The big one was wrecked near those same islands of Cyprus, and only the people escaped; in the same storm the Turkish ship was lost and all the people with it. The small vessel had great trouble, but in the end they reached land somewhere in

Apulia. This was in the depth of winter, and it was very cold and snowing. The pilgrim had no clothing other than some breeches of coarse cloth — knee-length and legs bare — with shoes and a doublet of black cloth, opened by many slashes at the shoulders, and a jacket that was short and quite thin.

50   He arrived in Venice in mid-January of the year '24, having been at sea from Cyprus the whole months of November and December and what was gone of January. In Venice, one of the two who had welcomed him in their homes before he set out for Jerusalem, met him and gave him as alms fifteen or sixteen *giulii* and a piece of cloth, which he folded many times and put over his stomach because of the great cold.

    After the pilgrim realized that it was not God's will that he remain in Jerusalem, he continually pondered within himself what he ought to do; and eventually he was rather inclined to study for some time so he would be able to help souls, and he decided to go to Barcelona. So he set out from Venice for Genoa. One day, whilst going through his devotions in the principal church of Ferrara, a beggar asked him for alms and he gave him a *marchetto*, which is a coin of five or six *quatrini*. After that another came, and he gave him another small coin that he had, somewhat larger; and to a third he gave a *giulio*, having nothing but *giulii*. The beggars, seeing that he was giving alms, kept coming and so all he had was finished. Finally, many beggars came together seeking alms. His response was to ask pardon, as he had nothing left.

51 So he left Ferrara for Genoa. On the road he met some Spanish soldiers who treated him well that night; but they were much surprised that he travelled that road, because one had to pass practically between the two armies, the French and the Imperial. They urged him to leave the highway and to take another safe road that they showed him. But he did not take their advice. Instead, travelling straight on he came upon a burned and destroyed village; and so till night he found no one to give him anything to eat.

But at sunset he reached a walled place where the guards immediately seized him, thinking he was a spy. They put him in a cabin next to the gate and began to question him, as is usual when there is some suspicion, but he replied to all their questions that he knew nothing. They stripped him and searched him down to his shoes, and all over his body, to see if he was carrying any letters. Unable to learn anything by any means, they took hold of him that he might appear before the captain — he would make him talk. He asked them to take him clothed in his jacket, but they refused to give it to him and took him in the breeches and doublet mentioned above.

52 On the way the pilgrim had some sort of impression of when Christ was led away, but this was not a vision like the others. He was led through three main streets, and he went without any

sadness, but rather with joy and satisfaction. It was his custom to speak to any person, no matter who it might be, using "you," piously holding that Christ and the apostles had spoken in this way, etc. As he was going thus through the streets, it crossed his fancy that it would be wise to give up that custom in this situation and address the captain as "Sir." This because of some fear of the tortures they might inflict, etc. But recognizing that this was a temptation, "Since it is such," he said, "I will not address him as Sir nor do him reverence nor take off my cap to him."

53 They reached the captain's headquarters and left him in a lower room. A while later the captain spoke to him. Without using any form of courtesy, he answered in a few words, with a noticeable interval between one and the next. The captain took him for a madman and said so to those who had brought him: "This man is not in his senses. Give him his things and throw him out." Just on leaving the headquarters he met a Spaniard who lived there; he took him to his house and gave him something to break his fast and all the necessaries for that night.

Setting out in the morning, he travelled until evening, when two soldiers in a tower saw him and came down to seize him. They took him to their captain, who was French; the captain asked him, among other things, from what country he came, and learning that he was from Guipúzcoa, he said to him, "I come from near there," apparently from near Bayonne. Then he said, "Take him and give him supper and treat him well." On this road from Ferrara to Genoa he had many other little experiences.

At last he reached Genoa where a Vizcayan named Portundo, who had spoken with him on other occasions when he served in the court of the Catholic King, recognized him. This man got him passage on a ship going to Barcelona, in which he ran great danger of being captured by Andrea Doria, who gave chase, being then on the French side.

CHAPTER 6
ONWARDS TO ALCALÁ
1524-1527

The illustration presents a view of the hospice of Antezana in Alcalá, where Ignatius was charitably accommodated.

6

54 When he arrived at Barcelona he made his wish to study known to Isabel Roser and to a Master Ardévol who taught grammar. To both this seemed a very good idea; he offered to teach him for nothing, and she to give him what he needed to support himself. In Manresa the pilgrim had known a friar (of the order of St. Bernard, I think), a very spiritual man; he wanted to be with this person to learn and to be able to give himself more easily to the spirit, as also to be of help to souls. So he replied that he would accept the offer if he did not find in Manresa the facilities he was looking for. But when he went there, he found that the friar was dead.

So, returning to Barcelona, he began to study with great diligence. But one thing was very much in his way; there came to him new insights into spiritual matters and fresh relish, to such an extent that he could not memorize, nor could he drive them away no matter how much he resisted.

55 So, thinking often about this, he said to himself,

"Not even when I engage in prayer and am at Mass do such vivid insights come to me." Thus, little by little, he came to realize that this was a temptation. After praying he went to Our Lady of the Sea, near the master's house, having asked that he kindly listen to him just a while in that church. So when they were seated, he told him exactly all that went on in his soul and what little progress he had made until then for that reason; but he promised this same master, saying: "I promise you never to fail to listen to you these two years, so long as I can find bread and water in Barcelona with which I might support myself." As he made this promise with great determination, he never again had those temptations. The stomach pain that afflicted him in Manresa, for which reason he wore shoes, was gone, and he had felt well in the stomach ever since he set out for Jerusalem. For this reason, while he was studying at Barcelona, he had the desire to resume his previous penances and so he began to make a hole in the soles of his shoes, which he kept widening little by little so that when the winter cold came, he was wearing only the uppers.

56 After two years of study during which, so they said, he had made great progress, his master informed him he could now study the liberal arts and should go to Alcalá. Even so, he had himself examined by a doctor of theology who gave him the same advice. So he set out alone for Alcalá: though he already had some companions, I think.

When he arrived at Alcalá, he began to beg

and to live on alms. After he had lived in this fashion for ten or twelve days, a cleric and others who were with him, seeing him beg alms one day, began to laugh at him and to utter some insults, as one usually does to those who, being healthy, go begging. At that moment the superintendent of the new hospice of Antezana passed by, and expressing regret at this, called him and took him to the hospice where he gave him a room and all he needed.

57 He ṣtudied at Alcalá almost a year and a half. Since he had arrived in Barcelona in the year '24 during Lent, and had studied there for two years, it was in the year '26 that he reached Alcalá. He studied the logic of Soto, the physics of Albert, and the Master of the Sentences. While at Alcalá, he was engaged in giving spiritual exercises and teaching Christian doctrine, and this bore fruit for the glory of God. There were many persons who came to a deep understanding and relish of spiritual things; but others had various temptations — there was one such who wanted to take the discipline but could not do so, as though the hand were held, and other similar cases. These gave rise to talk among the people, especially because of the great crowd that gathered wherever he was explaining doctrine.[8]

Soon after he arrived in Alcalá, he became ac-

---

[8] I will recall the fright that he himself got one night.

quainted with Don Diego de Guia who was staying with his brother, a printer in Alcalá, who was
quite well off. So they helped him with alms to
support the poor. The pilgrim's three companions
were lodged in his house. Once when he came to
ask alms for some needs, Don Diego said he had
no money, but he opened for him a chest in
which he had various objects, and then gave him
bed coverings of different colours and some
candlesticks and suchlike things. Wrapping them
all in a sheet, the pilgrim put them on his
shoulders and went off to aid the poor.

58 As mentioned above, there was much talk
throughout that region about the things happen-
ing at Alcalá; some spoke one way, some another.
The thing reached the inquisitors at Toledo.
When these came to Alcalá, the pilgrim was
alerted by their host, who told him that they were
calling them "ensayalados" and, I believe, "alumbrados," and that they would butcher them. So
they began at once to investigate and examine
their life; but finally they returned to Toledo
without summoning them, though they had come
for that sole purpose.

They left the trial to the vicar Figueroa, who
is now with the Emperor. A few days later he
summoned them and told them how an investigation and examination of their life had been made
by the inquisitors and that no error had been
found in their teaching nor in their life, and
therefore they could go on doing the same as they

did without any hindrance. But since they were not religious, it did not seem right for them to go about all in the same habit. It would be well, and he so ordered, that two of them, pointing to the pilgrim and Arteaga, dyed their clothes black; and that the other two, Calixto and Cáceres, dyed theirs brown; Little John, who was a French lad, could stay as he was.

59 The pilgrim says they will do what they are ordered. "But," he says, "I do not know what benefit these inquisitions bring; the other day a priest did not want to give the sacrament to someone because he went to communion every eight days; and they were objecting to me, too. We would like to know if they have found any heresy in us." "No," says Figueroa, "for if they did, they would burn you." "They would burn you too," says the pilgrim, "if they found heresy in you." They dye their clothing, as they are ordered, and fifteen or twenty days later, Figueroa orders the pilgrim not to go barefoot but to wear shoes; and so he does without fuss, as in all matters of this sort that he was ordered.

Four months later Figueroa himself again began an investigation of them. Besides the usual reasons, I believe this was also something of a factor, that a married woman of rank had special regard for the pilgrim. In order not to be noticed, she came to the hospice at dawn, wearing a veil, as is the custom in Alcalá de Henares. On entering she removed her veil and went to the pilgrim's room. But they did nothing to them this time either, nor did they say anything to them.[9]

60 After another four months, he being now in a cabin outside the hospice, a policeman came to his door one day and called him, saying, "Just come with me." He put him in jail and said to him, "You may not leave here until you are ordered otherwise." This was in the summertime, and as he was not confined, many people came to visit him.[10].

He did the same things as when he was free, teaching and giving exercises. Never would he have an advocate or attorney, though many offered themselves. He especially remembers Doña Teresa de Cárdenas who sent someone to visit him and frequently offered to get him out; but he accepted nothing, always answering, "He for whose love I got in here will get me out, if he is served thereby."

61 He was in prison seventeen days without being examined or knowing the reason for it. At the end of that time Figueroa came to the jail and examined him about many things, even asking him if he enjoined observance of the sabbath; and whether he knew two particular women, a mother and her daughter (and to this he said yes); whether he had known of their departure before they had set out

---

[9] R. what Bustamante told me.
[10] M^a one, and was confessor.

(and he said no, by the oath he had sworn). The vicar then placed a hand on his shoulder, manifesting joy, and said, "This is the reason why you were brought here."

Among the many persons who followed the pilgrim there were a mother and her daughter, both widowed. The daughter was very young and very attractive. They had made great spiritual progress, especially the daughter. So much so that though they were noble women, they had gone to the Veronica of Jaén on foot; possibly begging, and unaccompanied. This caused considerable gossip in Alcalá, and Doctor Ciruelo, who had some responsability for them, thought that the prisoner had persuaded them and for this reason had him arrested.

Having taken in the vicar's words, the prisoner said to him, "Would you like me to speak more at length about this affair?" He said, "Yes." "Then you should know," said the prisoner, "that these two women have often insisted with me that they wanted to go about the world serving the poor in one hospital and then in another. I have always dissuaded them from this plan, because the daughter is so young and so attractive, etc. And I have told them that when they wanted to visit the poor, they could do so in Alcalá, and could accompany the Blessed Sacrament." When this conversation was finished, Figueroa left with his notary, taking a complete written statement.

62 At that time Calixto was in Segovia, and learning

of his imprisonment came at once, though but recently recovered from a serious illness, and got into jail with him. He for his part suggested it would be better to go and call on the vicar — who received him kindly and manifested the intention to send him to jail, for that is where he had to be till those women returned, to see if they confirmed what had been said. Calixto remained in jail a few days, but when the pilgrim saw that this harmed his bodily health, because he was not yet entirely well, he had him released with the help of a doctor, a great friend of his.

From the day the pilgrim entered jail until they let him out, forty-two days passed. At the end of that time, as the two pious women returned, the notary came to the jail to read the sentence: he should go free; and they should dress like the other students, and should not speak about matters of faith until they had studied for four more years, because they had no education. For in truth, the pilgrim was the one who had the most, and that was with little foundation. This was the first thing he used to say whenever they examined him.

63   Because of this sentence he was somewhat doubtful what he should do, for seemingly they were closing the door for him to help souls, without giving him any reason except that he had not studied. At last he decided to go to Fonseca, the Archbishop of Toledo, and put the case in his hands. He set out from Alcalá and found the Archbishop in Valladolid. Faithfully recounting

the affair to him, he said that, even though he was not now in his jurisdiction nor obliged to abide by the sentence, still he would do whatever he commanded in this matter (he addressed him as "you" as was his custom with everyone). The Archbishop received him very well; adding he had friends and a college in Salamanca too, all of which he put at his disposal; and just as he was leaving, he had four *escudos* given to him.

CHAPTER 7
TROUBLES AT SALAMANCA
1527

The illustration shows a typical lecture room in the University of Salamanca, where Ignatius had wanted to study.

7

64 On arrival in Salamanca, while he was praying in a church, he was recognized by a devoted friend of the group — for his four companions had been there some days already. She asked him his name and then took him to the lodgings of his companions. When the sentence had been given in Alcalá that they should dress like students, the pilgrim said, "When you ordered us to dye our clothes, we did so; but now we cannot do this, because we do not have the means to buy them." So the vicar himself provided them with clothing and caps and all the other student gear. Dressed in this fashion they had left Alcalá.

At Salamanca he went to confession to a Dominican friar at St Stephen's. Ten or twelve days after his arrival the confessor said to him one day, "The fathers of the house would like to speak with you." He said, "In the name of God." "Then," said the confessor, "it would be well if you came here to dine on Sunday; but I warn you of one thing, that they will want to know many things from you." So on Sunday he came with Calixto.

After dinner, the subprior, in the absence of the prior, together with the confessor and I think with another friar, went with them to a chapel. With great cordiality the subprior began to say what good reports they had of their life and ways: that they went about preaching in apostolic fashion; and that they would be pleased to learn about these things in greater detail. So he began asking what they had studied. The pilgrim replied, "Of all of us, I am the one who has studied the most," and he gave a clear account of the little he had studied and with what little foundation.

65 "Well, then, what do you preach?" "We do not preach," said the pilgrim, "but we do speak familiarly with some people about the things of God; for example, after dinner with some people who invite us." "But," said the friar, "what things of God do you speak about? That is just what we would like to know." "We speak," said the pilgrim, "sometimes of one virtue, sometimes of another; and do so, praising it; sometimes of one vice, sometimes of another, condemning it." "You are not learned men," said the friar, "and you speak about virtues and vices; but no one can speak about these except in one of two ways: either through learning or through the Holy Spirit. If not through learning, then through the Holy Spirit."[11]

---

[11] What we wanted to know is this that comes from the Holy Spirit.

At this the pilgrim was somewhat on his guard, because that kind of argument did not seem good to him. After being silent a while, he said it was not necessary to speak further of these matters. The friar insisted, "Well, now that there are so many errors of Erasmus and of so many others who have deceived the world, you do not wish to explain what you say?"

66 The pilgrim said, "Father, I will say no more than I have said, except before my superiors who can oblige me to do so." Before this the friar had asked why Calixto came dressed as he was: he wore a short tunic and a large hat on his head, with a staff in his hand and boots almost halfway up the leg; and being very tall, he looked the more grotesque. The pilgrim related how they had been imprisoned in Alcalá and had been ordered to dress like students and that his companion, because of the great heat, had given his gown to a poor cleric. At this the friar seemed to mutter to himself indicating that he was not pleased, "Charity begins at home."

Well, getting back to the story: the subprior, unable to get any other word out of the pilgrim but that, said, "Then remain here, and we will indeed make you tell all." So all the friars left with some haste. The pilgrim first asked if they wanted them to remain in that chapel, or where did they want them to remain. The subprior answered that they should remain in the chapel. The friars then closed all the doors and, as it appears, took the matter up with the judges. Still the two of them were in the monastery for three days, eating in the refectory with the friars, without anything being said to them in the name of the court. Their room was almost always full of friars who came to see them. The pilgrim always spoke on his usual topics; as a result there was already some division among them, many showing that they were sympathetic.

67 At the end of three days a notary came and took them to jail. They were not put down below with the criminals but in an upper room where, because it was old and unused, there was much dirt. They were both bound with the same chain, each one by his foot. The chain was attached to a post in the middle of the house and would be ten or thirteen palms long. Each time that one wanted to do something, the other had to accompany him. All that night they kept awake. The next day, when their imprisonment was known in the city, people sent to the jail something on which they could sleep and all that was needed, in abundance. Many people came continually to visit them, and the pilgrim kept up his practice of speaking about God, etc.

The bachelor Frías came to examine each of them separately, and the pilgrim gave him all his papers, which were the Exercises, to be examined. Asked if they had companions, they said they did, and where they were. Straightaway some went there on the bachelor's orders and brought Cáceres and Arteaga to the jail; and they left Little John, who later became a friar. However they did not put them above with the other two but down where the common prisoners were. Here neither, would he have an advocate or attorney.

68 Some days later he was summoned before four judges: the three doctors, Sanctisidoro, Paravinhas, and Frías; and the fourth was the bachelor Frías. All of them had already seen the Exercises. Now they asked him many things not only about the Exercises, but also about theology; for example, about the Trinity and the Eucharist, and how he understood these articles. First he made his introduction; nevertheless, ordered by the judges, he spoke in such a manner that they had no reason to fault him. The bachelor Frías, who on these points had throughout been to the fore, also asked him about a canonical case. He was required to answer everything, but he always said first that he did not know what scholars said about those matters.

Then they ordered him to explain the first commandment in the way he usually explained it. He started to do so and took so long and said so many things about the first commandment that they were not inclined to ask him more. Before this, when they were speaking about the Exercises, they insisted a good deal on one point only in them, which was at the beginning: when a thought is a venial sin and when it is mortal. The question was why he, without studies, was deciding that. He answered, "If this is true or not: decide that; and if it is not true, condemn it." But in the end they left without condemning anything.

69   Among the many who came to speak to him in jail, once Don Francisco de Mendoza, who now has the title of Cardinal of Burgos, came with the bachelor Frías. In a friendly way he asked him how he was getting on in prison and if it bothered him to be imprisoned. He replied, "I will answer what I answered today,to a lady who, on seeing me in prison, spoke words of compassion. I said to her, 'By this you show that you do not wish to be imprisoned for the love of God. Does imprisonment seem to be such a great evil to you? Well, I will tell you that there are not so many fetters and chains in Salamanca that I do not want more for the love of God'."

At this time it happened that all the prisoners in the jail fled, but the two companions who were with them did not flee. In the morning when they were found there alone without anyone, with the doors open, all were deeply edified, and there was much talk in the city; so they gave them an entire mansion that was nearby, as a prison.

70   After twenty-two days of imprisonment, they were summoned to hear the sentence, which was that no error was found in their life or teaching. Therefore they could do what they had been doing, teaching doctrine and speaking about the things of God, so long as they never defined: this is a mortal sin or this is venial, until they had spent four years in further studies. After the sentence was read, the judges displayed great affection, apparently wishing to make it acceptable. The pilgrim said he would do everything the

sentence ordered, but he did not find it acceptable, because without condemning him for
anything they shut his mouth so he might not help
his neighbours in what he could. Although Doctor
Frías urged and showed himself very well dispos-
ed, the pilgrim said no more — only that as long
as he was in the jurisdiction of Salamanca he
would do what had been ordered.

Then they were released from jail, and he
began to commend the matter to God and to
think about what he ought to do. He found great
difficulty in remaining in Salamanca, for it seemed
to him that the door had been closed to helping
souls, by this prohibition not to determine mortal
and venial sin.

71 So he decided to go to Paris to study. When the
pilgrim was considering in Barcelona whether he
should study and how much, his one concern had
been whether, after he had studied, he would
enter a religious institute or go about the world.
When thoughts of entering an institute came to
him, then he also had the desire to enter a deca-
dent and not quite reformed one (if he were to be
a religious) so that he would suffer more in it;
and thinking also that perhaps God would help
them. And God gave him great confidence that he
would endure easily all the insults and injuries
they might inflict.

Now, at the time of his imprisonment in
Salamanca, he still felt the same desire that he had
to help souls, and for that reason to study first
and to gather some others with the same idea,

and to keep those he had. So he decided to go to Paris, and he arranged with them that they wait there while he went, to see if he could find some means by which they might study.

72 Many important persons urged strongly that he should not go, but they could never dissuade him. Rather, fifteen or twenty days after leaving prison, he set out alone, taking some books on a little donkey. When he arrived at Barcelona, all those who knew him advised him against the journey to France because of the fierce wars, recounting very specific instances, even telling him that they put Spaniards on spits; but he never had any kind of fear.

Chapter 8
PROGRESS IN PARIS
1528-1535

The illustration reproduces the diploma of Master of Arts that Ignatius received at the University of Paris.

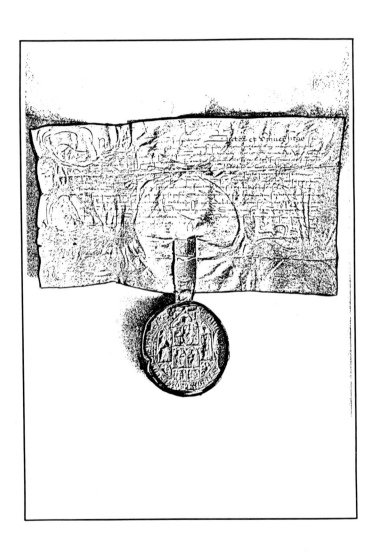

8

73 So he set out for Paris, alone and on foot. He reached Paris in the month of February, or thereabouts; and as he tells me, this was in the year 1528 or '27. He lodged in a house with some Spaniards and went to study humanities at Montaigu. The reason was that as they had made him advance with such haste in studies, he found himself very deficient in fundamentals. He studied with children following the order and method of Paris.[12]

When he first came to Paris, a merchant gave him twenty-five *escudos* on a draft from Barcelona; and these he gave to one of the Spaniards in those lodgings to keep; but in a short time the latter spent them and had not the means to pay him. So after Lent the pilgrim had nothing left, both because the other had spent the money

---

[12] When he was imprisoned in Àlcalá, the Prince of Spain was born; and from this one can calculate everything, even previous events.

and because of the reason mentioned above. He was compelled to beg and even to leave the house where he was staying.

74 He got admission into the hospice of St James, beyond the Innocents. He was greatly inconvenienced in study because the hospice was a good distance from the college of Montaigu, and in order to find the door open one had to return at the sound of the Angelus and to leave in daylight. Thus he could not attend his classes properly. Having to beg alms to support himself was another obstacle.

It was almost five years now that he felt no stomach pains, so he began to subject himself to greater penances and fasts. After some time, in this life of hospice and begging, seeing that he was making little progress in studies, he began to consider what he should do. Seeing that there were several who served some of the regents in the colleges and had time to study, he decided to seek a master.

75 He found great consolation in the following reflection and resolution which he entertained, imagining that the master would be Christ, that one of the students he would call St Peter and another St John, and so with each one of the apostles: "When the master orders me, I will think that Christ orders me; when another orders me, I will think that St Peter orders me." He tried hard to find a master; for one thing, he spoke to the bachelor Castro; and also to a Carthusian friar

who knew many teachers, and to others; but never could they find him a master.

76 At last, as he found no solution, a Spanish friar told him one day that it would be better for him to go each year to Flanders and spend two months or even less, to secure the means to study the whole year. After commending this to God, it seemed good to him. Following this advice, each year he brought back from Flanders enough to carry on in some way. Once he also went over to England and fetched more alms than he usually did in other years.

77 The first time he returned from Flanders he got more involved than usual in spiritual contacts, and he gave exercises almost simultaneously to three persons, namely, Peralta, the bachelor Castro who was at the Sorbonne, and a Vizcayan named Amador, who was at St Barbara. These were quite transformed and so gave all they had to the poor, even their books, and began to beg alms through Paris. They went to lodge in the hospice of St James, where the pilgrim had stayed before but which he had now left for the reasons mentioned above.

This caused great commotion in the university, for the first two were distinguished persons and well known. The Spaniards then began a campaign against the two masters; but not being able to convince them with much argument and persuasion, that they return to the university, one day many went armed and dragged them out of the hospice.

78 When they were brought to the university, an agreement was arrived at, that after they had finished their studies, then they would carry out their plans. The bachelor Castro later came to Spain and preached at Burgos for some time, and then became a Carthusian friar in Valencia. Peralta set out on foot as a pilgrim to Jerusalem. In these circumstances he was captured in Italy by a captain, a relative of his, who took steps to bring him to the Pope, whom he got to order him to return to Spain. These things did not happen immediately but some years later.

Great complaints arose in Paris, especially among the Spaniards, against the pilgrim. Our Master de Gouvea, saying that he had caused Amador, who was in his college, to go mad, decided and stated that the first time he came to St Barbara he would subject him to a drubbing as a seducer of the students.

79 The Spaniard with whom he had stayed at the beginning and who had spent his money, without paying it back set out for Spain by way of Rouen. While awaiting passage at Rouen, he fell sick. While he was thus ill, the pilgrim learned this from a letter of his and felt the desire to visit and help him. He also thought that in those circumstances he could win him over to leave the world and give himself completely to the service of God.

In order to achieve this he felt the desire to walk the twenty-eight leagues from Paris to Rouen barefoot, without eating or drinking. As he prayed over this, he felt very afraid. At last he went to St Dominic's, and there he decided to go in the manner just mentioned, the great fear he had of tempting God having now passed.

He got up early the next day, the morning that he was going to set out. As he began to dress, such a great fear came over him that he seemed almost unable to dress himself. In spite of that repugnance he left the house, and the city too, before it was quite daylight. Still the fear was with him constantly and persisted as far as Argenteuil, a walled town three leagues from Paris on the way to Rouen, where the garment of Our Lord is said to be. He passed the town with that spiritual distress, but as he came up to a rise the thing began to go away. He felt great consolation and spiritual strength, with such joy that he began to shout through the fields and to speak to God, etc.

He lodged that evening with a poor beggar in a hospice, having travelled fourteen leagues that day. The next day he sought shelter in a barn. The third day he reached Rouen: all this time without eating or drinking and barefoot, as he had determined. In Rouen he consoled the sick man and helped him board a ship to go to Spain. He also gave him letters directing him to the companions who were in Salamanca, namely, Calixto, Cáceres, and Arteaga.

80　Not to have to speak further of these companions, their lot was this: while the pilgrim was in Paris he wrote frequently to them, as they had agreed—about the scant facilities he had to bring them to Paris to study. Still, he undertook to write to Dona Leonor de Mascarenhas to assist Calixto with letters to the court of the King of Portugal, so he could obtain one of the scholarships which the King of Portugal gave in Paris. Dona Leonor gave Calixto the letters and a mule to ride and money for his expenses. Calixto went to the court of the King of Portugal, but in the end he did not come to Paris; rather, returning to Spain he went to the Imperial Indies with a certain spiritual woman. He returned to Spain later but went to the same Indies once more and this time returned to Spain a rich man, surprising all in Salamanca who had known him before.

Cáceres returned to Segovia, which was his hometown, and there began to live in such a manner that he seemed to have forgotten his earlier resolution.

Arteaga was made a *comendador*. Later when the Society was already in Rome, he was offered a bishopric in the Indies. He wrote to the pilgrim that he give it to one of the Society, but the answer was in the negative, so he went to the Imperial Indies as a bishop and died there in strange circumstances; that is, when he happened to be ill, there were two water bottles to refresh him, one with water which the doctor had ordered for him, the other with Water of Soliman, a poison—the later was given him by mistake and killed him.

81   The pilgrim returned to Paris from Rouen and discovered that because of the affair of Castro and Peralta there was much talk regarding him and that the inquisitor had issued a summons for him. But he would not wait further and went to the inquisitor, to whom he said that he understood he was looking for him, and that he was prepared for anything he might wish (the inquisitor was Our Master Ory, a Dominican friar), but he would request that he expedite it, because he had in mind to enroll in the arts course the coming St Remy's; he wanted to get this business over first so he would be better able to attend to his studies. The inquisitor did not summon him further, only telling him it was true that they had spoken of his doings, etc.

82   A short time after this came St Remy's, that is, the first of October, and he enrolled in the arts course under a teacher named Master Juan Peña—enrolled with the idea of retaining those who had decided to serve the Lord, but not to go farther in search of others, so that he could study more easily.

As he began attending the lectures of the course, the same temptations began to come to him that had come when he studied grammar in Barcelona. Whenever he was at a lecture, he could not pay attention because of the many spiritual thoughts that came to him. Realizing that in this way he made little progress in study, he went to his master and promised he would never fail to follow the whole course, so long as he could find bread and water for his sustenance. After making this promise, all that devotion which came to him out of time left him, and he went on quietly with his studies.

At this time he associated with Master Peter Faber and Master Francis Xavier, whom he later won for God's service by means of the Exercises.

At that stage in his course they did not harass him as before. With reference to this, Doctor Frago once told him how he marvelled that he went about so peacefully, without anyone giving him trouble; and he replied, "The reason is because I do not speak to anyone of the things of God; but once the course is over, we'll be back to business as usual."

83 While the two were speaking together, a friar came to ask Doctor Frago that he try to find him a house, because in the one where he had lodging, many people had died—of the plague, he thought; for the plague was then beginning in Paris. Doctor Frago and the pilgrim wished to go to see the house. They took a woman well versed in these matters, and on entering in she confirmed that it was the plague. The pilgrim also chose to enter. Coming upon a sick person, he comforted him and touched his sore with his hand.

After he had comforted and encouraged him a while, he went off alone. His hand began to hurt so that it seemed he had caught the plague. This fancy was so strong that he could not overcome it until he thrust his hand forcefully into his mouth and moved it about inside, saying, "If you have the plague in the hand, you will also have it in the mouth." When he had done this, he was rid of the fancy and of the pain in the hand.

84 But when he returned to the college of St Barbara where he then had lodging and was attending the course, those in the college who knew that he had entered the plague-ridden house, fled from him and would not let him enter. So he was forced to remain out for some days.

It is the custom in Paris for those who are studying arts in the third year, in order to receive the baccalaureate, "to take a stone," as they say. And because one has to spend an *escudo* for that, those who are very poor cannot do so. The pilgrim began to wonder whether it would be good for him to take it. Finding himself in great doubt and undecided, he determined to put the matter in the hands of his master, who advised him to take it, and he did so. There were not lacking, however, some critics—at least one Spaniard who commented upon it.

In Paris already by this time he was quite unwell in the stomach, so that every fifteen days he had a stomach-ache which lasted over an hour and gave him a fever. Once the stomach-ache lasted sixteen or seventeen hours. At this time he had already finished the arts course and studied theology for some years, and gathered the companions. His trouble kept getting worse and worse, and he could not find a cure, though many were tried.

85 The doctors said there was nothing left that might help him except his native air—just that. Moreover, the companions gave him the same advice and pressed him hard. Already by this time they had all determined what they would do, namely, go to Venice and to Jerusalem, and spend their lives for the good of souls; and if they were not given permission to remain in Jerusalem, then return to Rome and present themselves to the Vicar of Christ, so that he could make use of them wherever he thought it would be more for the glory of God and the good of souls. They also planned to wait a year in Venice for passage; but if there was no passage for the East that year, they would be free of their vow about Jerusalem and approach the Pope, etc.

In the end, the pilgrim let himself be persuaded by the companions, and also because the Spaniards among them had some business which he could settle. It was agreed that when he felt well he should go and attend to their business, and then proceed to Venice where he would wait for the companions.

86 This was the year '35, and the companions were to set out, according to the agreement, in the year '37 on the day of the conversion of St Paul; though in fact, because of the outbreak of war, they eventually left in November of the year '36.

As the pilgrim was about to set out, he learned that he had been accused before the inquisitor, with a case brought against him. Knowing this but seeing that they did not summon him, he went to the inquisitor and told him what he had heard and that he was about to set out for Spain and that he had companions. Would he please pass sentence. The inquisitor said it was true there was an accusation, but that he did not find anything of importance in it. He only wanted to see his manuscript of the Exercises. When he saw it he praised it very much and asked the pilgrim to let him have the copy; and he did so. Nevertheless, he again insisted that the case be carried through to the sentence. As the inquisitor excused himself, he brought a public notary and witnesses to his house, and obtained a testimonial on this whole affair.

Chapter 9
FAREWELL TO SPAIN
1535

The illustration shows the great Basilica built in Loyola by the side of the castle, long after Ignatius passed that way.

9

87   With that done, he mounted a pony the companions had bought him and set out alone homewards. Along the way he felt much better. When he arrived in the Province, he left the highway and took the mountain road, which was more secluded. Having moved along a bit, he saw two armed men who were approaching him (that road is somewhat notorious for assassins). A little after they had passed him, they turned about and came toward him in great haste, and he was a little afraid. All the same he spoke to them, and learned that they were servants of his brother, who had sent them to meet him; because, as it seems, he had had news of his coming from Bayonne in France, where the pilgrim was recognized.

So they went ahead, and he went the same way. Just before he got to the place, he came upon the above-mentioned men, who were approaching him. They were very insistent about taking him to his brother's house, but they could not constrain him. So he went to the hospice and later at a convenient hour went to seek alms in the locality.

88 In this hospice he began to speak with many who came to visit him, of the things of God, and by his grace much fruit was derived. As soon as he arrived, he decided to teach Christian doctrine every day to children, but his brother strongly objected to this, saying that no one would come. He replied that one would be enough. But after he began to do it, many came continually to hear him; and even his brother.

Besides Christian doctrine, he also preached on Sundays and feasts, with profit and help to the souls who came many miles to hear him. He also made an attempt to eliminate some abuses, and with God's help some were set right. For example, he persuaded the one administering justice to have an effective ban on gambling. There was also another abuse there; namely, the girls in that region always go about with head uncovered and do not cover it until they are married. But there are many who have become concubines of priests and other men, and are faithful to them as though they were their wives. This is so common that the concubines are not at all ashamed to say that they have covered their heads for so and so, and are acknowledged as such.

89 Much evil results from this custom. The pilgrim persuaded the governor to make a law that all those who covered the head for anyone, and were not the wives, should be legally punished. And so

this abuse began to be corrected. He got an order to be given that the poor should be provided for officially and regularly; and that bells should be rung three times at the Angelus, that is, morning, noon and evening, so that the people might pray as in Rome.

But though he had felt well at the beginning, he later fell seriously ill. Once he had recovered, he decided to set out to attend to the affairs his companions had entrusted to him, and to set out without money. At this his brother was very upset, and ashamed that he should go on foot. By evening the pilgrim was willing to settle for this: to go on horseback with his brother and his relatives to the border of the Province.

90 But when he left the Province he got to his feet without taking anything and went towards Pamplona, and thence to Almazán, Father Lainez's home; and then to Sigüenza and Toledo and from Toledo to Valencia. In all these native places of his companions he would not take anything, although they offered him much with great insistence.

In Valencia he spoke with Castro who was a Carthusian monk. He wanted to sail to Genoa but good friends in Valencia begged him not to do so, because they said Barbarossa was on the sea with many ships, etc. Although they did say many things, enough to frighten him, nevertheless nothing made him hesitate.

91 Boarding a large ship, he passed through the

storm mentioned above, when it was said that he was on the point of death three times.

When he arrived at Genoa he took the road to Bologna, on which he suffered much, especially once when he lost his way and began to walk by a river, which was down below whilst the way was up above, and became ever more narrow the farther he went along it. And it got so narrow that he could no longer go forward nor turn back. So he began to crawl along and in this way he covered a great distance in great fear, because each time he moved he thought he would fall into the river. This was the greatest physical stress and strain that he ever experienced, but finally he got through.

Making his way into Bologna and having to cross over a wooden footbridge, he fell off the bridge. Then, as he got up covered with mud and water, he made many bystanders laugh. Entering Bologna he began to beg alms, but not one small coin did he get though he sought everywhere. He was ill for some time in Bologna, but afterwards he went on to Venice, always in the same fashion.

Chapter 10
VENICE AND VICENZA
1535-1537

The illustration presents a view of modern Venice, with the characteristic features that have distinguished the city for centuries.

10

92 During that time in Venice, he busied himself giving the Exercises and in other spiritual contacts. The most distinguished persons to whom he gave them were Master Pietro Contarini and Master Gaspar de Doctis, and a Spaniard whose name was Rozas. There was also another Spaniard there called the bachelor Hoces, who was in close touch with the pilgrim and also with the bishop of Cette. Although he had some desire to make the Exercises, still he did not put it into execution.

At last he decided to begin making them. And having made them for three or four days, he spoke his mind to the pilgrim, telling him that because of the things someone had told him, he had been afraid that he would be taught some evil doctrine in the Exercises. For this reason he had brought with him certain books so he could have recourse to them, if perchance he tried to deceive him. He was helped very much by the Exercises and in the end resolved to live the pilgrim's way. He was also the first one to die.

93 In Venice the pilgrim also endured another persecution, with many saying that his effigy had been burned in Spain and in Paris. This business went so far that a trial was held and sentence was given in favour of the pilgrim.

The nine companions came to Venice at the beginning of '37. There they separated to serve in various hospices. After two or three months, they all went to Rome to obtain the blessing for the journey to Jerusalem. The pilgrim did not go because of Doctor Ortiz and also because of the new Theatine cardinal. The companions returned from Rome with drafts for 200 or 300 *escudos*, which had been given to them as alms for the journey to Jerusalem. They did not want to take anything except in drafts; later, not being able to go to Jerusalem, they gave them back to the donors.

The companions returned to Venice in the fashion they had gone, that is, on foot and begging, but divided into three groups and in such a way that they were always of different nationalities. There in Venice, those who were not ordained were ordained priests, and the Nuncio who was then in Venice (and who was later known as Cardinal Verallo) gave them faculties. They were ordained *ad titulum paupertatis* and all made vows of chastity and poverty.

94 In that year no ships sailed for the East because the Venetians had broken with the Turks. So, seeing that their hope of sailing was put off, they dispersed within the Venetian region, with the in-

tention of waiting the year they had decided upon; and if it expired without possibility of travel, they would go to Rome.

It fell to the pilgrim to go with Faber and Lainez to Vicenza. There they found a certain house outside the city, which had neither doors nor windows. They stayed in it, sleeping on a little straw that they had brought. Two of them always went out to seek alms in the city twice a day, but they got so little they could hardly maintain themselves. They usually ate a little toasted bread when they had it, and the one who remained at home saw to its toasting. In this way they spent forty days, not engaging in anything other than prayer.

95　After the forty days, Master John Codure arrived; and the four together decided to begin to preach. The four went to different piazzas and began to preach on the same day and at the same hour, first shouting loudly and summoning the people with their caps. Their preaching caused a great stir in the city, and many persons were moved with devotion, and they received in greater abundance the material goods they needed.

During the time he was at Vicenza, he had many spiritual visions and many quite regular consolations; the contrary happened when he was in Paris. In all that travelling he had great supernatural experiences like those he used to have when he was in Manresa, especially when he began to prepare for the priesthood in Venice and when he was preparing to say Mass.

While he was still at Vicenza, he learned that one of the companions, who was at Bassano, was ill to the point of death; at the same time he too was ill with fever. Nevertheless. he set out and walked so vigorously that Faber, his companion, could not keep up with him. On that journey he had assurance from God, and he told Faber so, that the companion would not die of that illness. On their arriving at Bassano, the sick man was much comforted and soon recovered. Then they all returned to Vicenza; and all ten were there for some time, and some used to go seeking alms in the towns around Vicenza.

96 Then, the year being over and no passage available, they decided to go to Rome—even the pilgrim, because on the other occasion when the companions had gone, those two about whom he had doubts had shown themselves very kind. Divided into three or four groups, the pilgrim with Faber and Lainez, they went to Rome. On this journey he was visited very especially by God.

He had decided to spend a year without saying Mass after he became a priest, preparing himself and praying Our Lady to deign to place him with her Son. One day, a few miles before reaching Rome, he was at prayer in a church and experienced such a change in his soul and saw so clearly that God the Father placed him with Christ his Son that he would not dare doubt it—that God the Father had placed him with his Son.[13]

97 Then on arriving in Rome he told the companions that he saw the windows were closed, meaning to say that they would have to meet many contradictions. He also said, "We must be very much on our guard, and not have contacts with women, unless they are prominent." While on this subject, later in Rome Master Francis was confessor to a woman and sometimes visited her to treat of spiritual matters, and she was subsequently found to be pregnant; but the Lord deigned that the one who had done the mischief should be discovered. The same sort of thing happened to John Codure, with a spiritual daughter who was caught with a man.

---

[13] And I who am writing these things, said to the pilgrim, when he told me this, that Lainez recounted it with other details—so I understood. He told me that everything that Lainez said was true, because he did not recall it in such detail, but that at the moment when he narrated it he was certain that he had said nothing but the truth. He said the same to me about other things.

CHAPTER 11
FINALLY IN ROME
1538

The illustration shows the features preserved in a mask made of the face of Ignatius as it rested in death.

11

98　From Rome the pilgrim went to Monte Cassino to give the Exercises to Doctor Ortiz. He was there forty days, and on one of them he saw the bachelor Hoces as he entered heaven. This brought him many tears and great spiritual consolation. He saw this so clearly that if he said the contrary he would feel he was lying. From Monte Cassino he brought with him Francis de Strada; and returning to Rome he busied himself helping souls. They were still living at the vineyard. He gave the Spiritual Exercises to various people at the same time, one of whom lived at Saint Mary Major, the other at Ponte Sesto.

Then the persecutions began. Miguel began to give trouble and to speak badly of the pilgrim, who caused him to be summoned before the governor. He first showed the governor a letter of Miguel's, in which he praised the pilgrim very much. The governor examined Miguel, and ended by banishing him from Rome.

Mudarra and Barreda then began their persecution, saying that the pilgrim and his companions were fugitives from Spain, from Paris, and from Venice. In the end both of them confessed in the presence of the governor and the legate, who was then in Rome, that they had nothing bad to say about them, neither regarding their ways nor regarding their teaching. The legate ordered silence to be imposed on the whole affair, but the pilgrim did not accept that, saying he wanted a definite sentence. This did not please the legate nor the governor nor even those who at first favoured the pilgrim; but at last, after some months, the Pope came to Rome. The pilgrim went to speak to him at Frascati and gave him several reasons; thus informed, the pope ordered sentence to be given, and it was given in his favour, etc.

With the help of the pilgrim and his companions some pious works such as the Catechumens, Saint Martha, the Orphans, etc., were begun in Rome.

Master Nadal can recount the rest.

99   After these things had been recounted, I asked the pilgrim on October 20 about the Exercises and the Constitutions, as I wanted to know how he had drawn them up. He told me that he had not composed the Exercises all at once, but that when he noticed some things in his soul and found them useful, he thought they might also be useful to others, and so he put them in writing; for example, the examination of conscience with that arrangement of lines, etc. He told me that he derived the elections in particular from that diversity of

spirit and thoughts which he had at Loyola when he was still suffering in the leg. He told me he would speak to me about the Constitutions in the evening.

The same day he summoned me before supper, with the air of a person who was more recollected than usual, and made a sort of protestation to me, the sum of which was to show the intention, the sincerity with which he had related these things. He said he was quite sure that he had not exaggerated; and that he had committed many offences against Our Lord after he began to serve him, but that he had never consented to mortal sin. Rather, he had always grown in devotion, that is, ease in finding God; and now more than ever in his whole life. Every time, any hour, that he wished to find God, he found him. And even now he often had visions, especially those mentioned above in which he saw Christ as the sun. This often happened while he was engaged in important matters, and that gave him confirmation.

100 He also had many visions when he said Mass; and when he was drawing up the Constitutions too, he had them very often. He can now affirm this more easily because every day he wrote down what went on in his soul and he had it now in writing. He then showed me a rather large bundle of writings, of which he read me a good bit. Most were visions that he saw in confirmation of some of the Constitutions, at times seeing God the Father, at times all three Persons of the Trinity; at

times Our Lady—who interceded and at times confirmed.

In particular he spoke to me about precisions over which he spent forty days, saying Mass each day, and each day with many tears. The question was whether a church would have any income and whether the Society should make use of that.

101 The method which he followed while he was drafting the Constitutions was to say Mass each day and to present to God the point that he was treating, and to pray over it; he always had tears at prayer and Mass.

I wished to see all those papers on the Constitutions, and asked him to let me have them a while; he would not.

NOTES

ACKNOWLEDGEMENTS
by the translator

Whatever merit this work may have is due in largest measure to the facilities available at the Jesuit Headquarters in Rome, chief among which were the generosity and competence of many colleagues who helped in many ways. The following were significantly involved in the actual work of translation:

Nicolás Rodríguez Verástegui and John P. Leonard; Bernard Hall and Gerald R. Sheahan.

To one and all, and to the Giver of all good gifts, thanks!

NOTES ON THE TEXT

The Memoirs of Ignatius of Loyola can best be understood in modern terms as an effort on his part, in response to pressing requests from the first Jesuits, to provide an insight into the charism of the Society of Jesus, as embodied in its founder. Viewed in this light his narrative manifests a remarkable coherence that is not immediately obvious; and one can even discern a pattern in what appears to be a haphazard account. It would be helpful to grasp the unifying idea, or the thread that runs through the text, so as to see each succeeding chapter in the right perspective.

What stands out in the whole story is that Ignatius had a veritable genius for loyalty—and almost a felt need to be loyal, to find a person or a cause that could claim his total devotion. As a young man he is constantly getting caught up in unrealistic ambitions, and not even the sobering experience of a shattered leg can break the spell. But some accidental reading reveals to him the true object of his quest: it is Christ, who alone is worthy of absolute loyalty and can satisfy the loftiest aspirations — in a way that is not self-centred but out-going.

In his encounter with Christ, Ignatius experiences loyalty as liberation. This paradox is the closest possible approach to a definition of the ignatian charism: loyalty is a firm attachment, something that binds; but loyalty to Christ is a liberation from all that hampers true and total growth. For through intimate union with Christ one comes to share his own experience— the experience that the man Jesus had of the Father, of God as Absolute and all else as relative. This is the truth that makes us free.

Chapter 1 shows the conversion of Ignatius as the discovery of a deeper and hitherto unsuspected level of being where his real self meets the real God in the person of Christ. It is a tremendously liberating experience; he feels an overwhelming desire to serve the Lord. But he is now firmly rooted in reality and cannot indulge in dreams; he must come to some concrete plan, whilst remaining open to other possibilities.

As the story proceeds, each succeeding situation he faces brings to him an ever clearer realization that commitment to Christ carries with it other commitments — which may seem to tie him down again, to be a restriction, but are experienced by him as a further release: new opportunities, calling forth fresh generosity. Loyalty to Christ means loyalty to the Church; loyalty to the Church means loyalty to the Pope... We thus come to three distinct phases in the subsequent narrative, each introduced by a brief chapter of transition, marking a new beginning and a more precise determination of his ideal of service.

Chapters 2 to 4: He sallies forth on a spiritual adventure under the patronage of the Virgin Mary. On the way, the Knight Errant is gradually transformed into a true Pilgrim—a humble seeker after the fullness of truth. In Manresa the Spirit leads him, through many trials and lessons, to a further profound experience of God as the one Reality embracing all reality. His journey to the homeland of Christ is a practical application of his new insight, through a complete abandonment to divine providence. He has an experience of the power of God at work in the destitute and the defenseless, and thus learns the secret of effectiveness in the service of the Kingdom.

Chapters 5 to 8: Without comment, he turns his back on his cherished plan of spending his life in the Holy Land, and makes a fresh start: he will study in order to prepare himself for a more universal apostolate in the Church. He moves through several great universities and learns much more than theology: he comes to understand the various hazards that attend the apostolic enterprise, and to appreciate better than ever that zeal for the truth must be fearless and not fearful; otherwise it does not lead to freedom but to an imprisoning of oneself and of others. Ignatius obeys all lawful authority in the Church, but refuses to surrender his liberty of spirit and his availability for the service of God's people.

Chapters 9 and 10: Another beginning, no longer of an individual but of a group, the Friends in the Lord whom Ignatius has gathered at the University of Paris and among whom he now assumes a definite leadership role. They bid farewell to their past and set their course eastwards for Jerusalem. But their destiny is in Rome, to be at the disposal of the Pope. As they approach the city, Ignatius has another deep experience of God in Christ, of the Father placing him with his Son. This is journey's end. The Pilgrim still has a long way to go, but that is no longer just his story; it is the history of the Society of Jesus.

The little band of newly ordained priests that came to offer their services to the Pope, had taken it for granted that once their resolution to make themselves available for the universal apostolate was fulfilled, their togetherness would end in dispersion. But at the very point of separation they were more conscious than ever that their companionship, their mutual loyalty, had been precisely the condition of their availability for service: the bond that held them together had never been a bondage but rather a liberation, the flowering of all that was noblest in them, of unsuspected qualities which the complementarity of their characters had brought out and fostered; it could also be the means to ensure that their services were in fact used to the best advantage.

So they decided to remain united, not only in spirit but also as members of a body. And the very thing they thought would scatter them—their commitment to the Pope—became "the starting point and main foundation" of a new religious order in the Church, mobile but close-knit. So the Society of Jesus was established on the principle of loyalty as liberation.

Chapter 11 then, concludes briefly with a glimpse of Ignatius as the Founder, drafting the Constitutions—but also bequeathing to his followers a Testament: his abiding sense of the presence of God; finding God in all things—which is the ultimate in loyalty and in liberation, till it finds its perfect fulfillment in eternity where God is all and in all.

There follow some more detailed explanations. The numbers refer to the corresponding numbers in the margin of the text, which are generally used in modern editions to facilitate consultation.

CHAPTER 1

1   The probable year of Ignatius' birth is 1491. He would be aged twenty-six when he entered the service of the Duke of Nájera, Antonio Manrique de Lara, who was Viceroy of Navarre under the Emperor Charles V. There are several references in the text to the struggle between the Emperor and the French King Francis I. But the wounding of Ignatius in the defence of Pamplona, capital of Navarre, with which his story begins, happened on May 20, 1521, when he must have been about thirty years old. He seems to have recounted some early escapades, whose omission from the text (on whose authority, it is not known) has disturbed the chronology.

2   The castle of Loyola, in the Basque province of Guipúzcoa, had been deprived of its upper storeys and warlike battlements, which were replaced by

a more peaceful and artistic construction in brick; on the top floor was the room occupied by Ignatius, later made into a chapel. The whole edifice is now surrounded by a basilica and other buildings.

5   The books given to Ignatius seem to have belonged to his sister-in-law Magdalena, who was something of a mother to him. The Life of Christ was by the Carthusian Ludolf of Saxony — in four volumes; the other book was the Flos Sanctorum or Golden Legend by the Dominican Bishop Jacobo de Varazze.

6   It has been impossible to determine the identity of the lady of the day-dreams. The best guess points to Princess Catalina, the charming younger sister of the Emperor Charles V, who was then in her early teens and later married King John III of Portugal, a generous patron of the Jesuits.

8   Here comes the first of thirteen marginal notes by da Camara, which are given in fine print at the bottom of the appropriate page. He speaks of *diversity of spirits*, and so does Ignatius; but it is rather a question of the *difference* between two spirits. It is generally understood that Ignatius says that the spirits were moving *him*, but the original uses the reflexive construction: *se agitaban*, which means simply that they were in motion, or *were stirring*.

12   The eldest Loyola brother, Juan Pérez, had died.
      The head of the family was now Martín García,
      referred to here, who was married to Magdalena
      de Araoz; he was much older than Iñigo, later
      known as Ignatius, who was the youngest; the
      brother in the next chapter was probably the
      priest, Pero López.

CHAPTER 2

13   Aránzazu was only a little hermitage at the time,
      but a popular shrine. There is now a big basilica
      and a large Franciscan establishment.

17   Amadis de Gaul is a mythical Prince of Wales,
      whose romantic story first appeared in 1508 and
      in eight years achieved an incredible thirtieth edi-
      tion; this led inevitably to a sequel on the son of
      Amadis, Esplandian, said to have been invested as
      a knight with a vigil of arms, before an image of
      the Virgin Mary. The confessor of the pilgrims
      was the saintly Frenchman Jean Chanon; he seems
      to have introduced Ignatius to the so-called
      Devotio Moderna, one of whose masterpieces is
      the Imitation of Christ, which he soon came to
      know and love.

18   The Black Virgin of Montserrat is one of the most
      famous Madonnas in the world, and the Benedic-
      tine monastery around it is a dearly loved place of
      pilgrimage, for nearly a thousand years.

Chapter 3

19   Manresa is a little town in the Spanish province of
      Catalonia, not exactly between Montserrat and
      Barcelona, but not far from either. It would seem
      that the long break in the dictation, mentioned by
      da Camara, occurred at the end of the previous
      chapter, though some place it in the middle of this
      one.

20   One can notice three phases in Ignatius' spiritual
      experience in Manresa: first he had peace, then
      trials, finally special graces and enlightenment.
      There is much in this chapter that illustrates what
      is said in the Spiritual Exercises, particularly
      about the discernment of spirits.

30   A great deal has been written about this ex-
      perience, which is regarded as of capital impor-
      tance in the life and work of Ignatius. But it re-
      mains veiled in mystery. It seems to have been a
      very privileged realization of God as he really is,
      embracing in himself all that is, so that the whole
      creation is seen in a new light and acquires a new
      meaning, which is its true meaning. This is later
      very baldly stated in the Spiritual Exercises as the
      Principle and Foundation.

34   Among the ladies attending on Ignatius was Inés
      Pascual, who became a close friend of his; she
      later gave him accommodation with her son dur-
      ing his stay in Barcelona, and the first of his many
      extant letters is addressed to her.

36   Here and in subsequent chapters, coins are mentioned, belonging to different currencies; they have been left as in the original unless there was a recognizable English equivalent. The "etc." that occurs here and elsewhere does not mean that something is omitted, but that Ignatius broke off the discourse.

CHAPTER 4

44   According to the punctuation that is adopted, Ignatius is either saying that his experience of Christ took place *after* he left Cyprus for Jaffa, or (as in our translation) stressing that he did not *actually* see Christ: he is meticulous in his statements.

48   Syrian Christians, who served in the convent, were known as "belted" because of the way they dressed.

CHAPTER 5

49   Rather characteristically, Ignatius has much to say of his journey to and from Palestine, and little of his experience in the Holy Land and at the sacred places. But two fellow pilgrims have left detailed accounts of the programme that was followed: the Swiss Peter Füssli and Philip Hagen from Strasbourg.

53   Ignatius was never directly in the service of the

Catholic King Ferdinand, but of his chief revenue officer, Juan Velázquez de Cuéllar, at Arévalo, before he went to serve under the Duke of Nájera.

Chapter 6

54 Isabel Roser, great friend and benefactress of Ignatius over the years, came to Rome and actually made the solemn profession in the Society of Jesus in 1545. Later she returned to Barcelona and joined a convent.

57 Diego de Eguía was related to Francis Xavier; he eventually entered the Society of Jesus and was confessor of Ignatius. The marginal notes in this chapter are not too clear: in the first we can only guess at some incident; the second seems to say: I will recall what Father Bustamante narrated; the third: Miona, who was his confessor, was among the visitors.

58 "Ensayalados" was just a nickname because Ignatius and his companions seemed to be wearing skirts. "Alumbrados" was a more serious matter, for that referred to an anti-institutional movement of people who claimed to be illumined, or guided interiorly, without regard for established authority.

Chapter 7

64 The opening lines are usually translated as if Ig-

natius had been recognized by a devout lady as belonging to the group. What the Spanish says is that he was recognized by a lady devoted to the group.

65 The Dominican convent of San Esteban was at that time the home of intellectual genius and great Christian charity; but it was also at the centre of a religious crisis, when the faith of Spain was threatened from various quarters. The treatment that Ignatius got is regrettable but not altogether surprising. A special cause of suspicion was the following that he attracted.

CHAPTER 8

73 Montagu was in several ways among the strictest of the fifty and more colleges of the University of Paris. Classes began at 5 a.m. Erasmus was here for some time, and then John Calvin. Ignatius later moved to St Barbara which was at the meeting point of the old scholasticism and the new humanism.

79 In the original text, the portion in Spanish ends with the first paragraph. Up to here the actual words of Ignatius are recorded, according to da Camara — who had to dictate the rest in such Italian as he could muster, when he stopped in Genoa on his way from Rome to Spain.

82 Pierre Favre, a Savoyard of humble origin, was

the first stable companion of Ignatius and the first priest of the Society of Jesus. Francisco Javier was a young noble from Navarre and his family was on the French side in the struggle in which Ignatius was wounded at Pamplona.

85   Here we find the gist of the special features in the vows made at Montmartre on August 15, 1534, by Ignatius and his first permanent companions: Xavier, Lainez, Favre, Salmeron, Bobadilla, Rodrigues. The ceremony marked the birth of the Company, later officially constituted as the Society of Jesus.

CHAPTER 9

87   The Province was Guipúzcoa, in which is the town of Azpeitia, where Loyola is situated. There is a pious tradition that Ignatius was solemnly received on arrival by the clergy. This seems based on a mistaken reading of the text: *preti* (priests) instead of *predetti* (above-mentioned).

89   There is a problem of punctuation: whether Ignatius was willing to settle *by evening*, or his brother was ashamed that he should go *in the evening*. We take the first alternative, as more likely.

Chapter 10

92   There is no diocese of Cette; probably Chieti is
     meant, whose Bishop Carafa, not too friendly
     with Ignatius, became the Theatine cardinal men-
     tioned later, and then Pope Paul IV.

93   To the six companions left in Paris, three others
     joined themselves: Le Jay, Broet and Codure.
     Favre was already a priest. Ignatius was ordained
     on June 24, 1537, with the others; but he waited
     till Christmas night of the following year for his
     first Mass.

96   The site of this very special experience has been
     reliably identified as La Storta, just outside Rome.
     The original chapel is no longer there and the pre-
     sent one is being renewed. The details recounted
     by Lainez have been cherished by Jesuits through
     the centuries, but seemingly for Ignatius they were
     all summed up in his being *placed with Christ*:
     this represents in some way the mature fruit of the
     Spiritual Exercises, just as the experience in
     Manresa corresponds to their starting point - ob-
     viously at a mystical depth not arrived at by the
     average retreatant.

Chapter 11

98   This chapter is made up of bits and pieces and the
     first section ends with a sign of relief, leaving the
     rest of the story to Nadal. Then da Camara takes

up the narrative, speaking in the first person and providing some very interesting and useful information.

100 The bundle of notes was destroyed by Ignatius; but a fragment has survived, and is now known and much appreciated as the Spiritual Diary; it includes the discernment of forty days on poverty, which is mentioned later.

TIPOGRAFIA P. U. G. - ROMA

STAMPA OFFSET